CW00429769

ISBN : 9798858362739
First edition, 2023

# Index

# Function #1 - CEILING

The `CEILING` function in Excel is designed to round numbers up, away from zero, to the nearest multiple of a given factor. This function can be particularly beneficial in various scenarios, such as:

1. **Financial Planning:** When you want to avoid fractions of cents in financial calculations.
2. **Inventory Management:** To round up order quantities to the nearest box or package size.
3. **Time Management:** To round up time entries to the nearest quarter or half-hour.
4. **Manufacturing:** To determine the number of materials needed, rounded up to whole units.

---

## Step-by-Step Guide

**Step 1:** Open your Excel workbook and navigate to the worksheet where you want to use the `CEILING` function.

**Step 2:** Click on the cell where you want the rounded result to appear.

**Step 3:** Enter the `CEILING` function. The syntax for the function is:

---

| **=CEILING(number, significance)** |
| --- |

- `number` is the value you want to round up.
- `significance` is the multiple to which you want to round up.

> ➤ **Depending on your country, the ' , ' must be replaced by ' ; '**

**Step 4**: After entering the required values, press `Enter`. Excel will display the rounded number in the selected cell.

---

## Example

**Downloadable example:**
https://tinyurl.com/102-excel-functions

Imagine you're a manufacturer who produces widgets. Each box can contain 8 widgets. You've received an order for 37 widgets. You want to determine how many full boxes you'll need to fulfill this order.

**Step 1:** Enter the number of widgets ordered in cell A1 (37 in this case).

**Step 2:** In cell B1, enter the number of widgets per box (8 in this case).

| ◢ | A | B | C |
|---|---|---|---|
| 1 | 37 | 8 | |
| 2 | | | |
| 3 | | | |

**Step 3:** In cell C1, enter the `CEILING` function to determine the number of boxes needed:

$$=\text{CEILING(A1/B1, 1)}$$

Step 4: Press `Enter`. Excel will display the result in cell C1. In this case, the result will be 5, meaning you'll need 5 full boxes to fulfill the order of 37 widgets.

| ◢ | A | B | C |
|---|---|---|---|
| 1 | 37 | 8 | 5 |
| 2 | | | |

**Note:** The `CEILING` function always rounds away from zero. If you're working with negative numbers, it will round them up (away from zero), making them more negative.

## Function #2 - ISODD

The `ISODD` function in Excel is used to test if a given number is odd. If the number is odd, the function returns `TRUE`, otherwise, it returns `FALSE`. This function can be particularly beneficial in various scenarios, such as:

1. **Data Validation:** Ensuring that a series of numbers meet certain criteria, like being odd.
2. **Mathematical Analysis:** Identifying odd numbers in a sequence or dataset.
3. **Game Development:** For games that require players to choose odd numbers.
4. **Pattern Recognition:** In scenarios where odd numbers might indicate a specific trend or anomaly.

---

## Step-by-Step Guide

**Step 1:** Open your Excel workbook and navigate to the worksheet where you want to use the `ISODD` function.

**Step 2:** Click on the cell where you want the result (TRUE or FALSE) to appear.

**Step 3:** Enter the `ISODD` function. The syntax for the function is:

---

**=ISODD(number)**

---

- `number` is the value you want to test.

**Step 4:** After entering the required number, press `Enter`. Excel will display `TRUE` if the number is odd and `FALSE` if it's not.

---

## Example:

**Downloadable example:**
https://tinyurl.com/102-excel-functions

Imagine you're a teacher and you've given your students a list of numbers. You want to identify which of these numbers are odd to create a pattern recognition exercise.

**Step 1:** Enter the list of numbers in column A, starting from A1. For instance:

A1: 5
A2: 12
A3: 7

A4: 8

A5: 19

| | A |
|---|---|
| 1 | 5 |
| 2 | 12 |
| 3 | 7 |
| 4 | 8 |
| 5 | 19 |

**Step 2:** In cell B1, enter the `ISODD` function to test the number in A1:

=ISODD(A1)

| | A | B |
|---|---|---|
| 1 | 5 | =ISODD(A1) |
| 2 | 12 | |
| 3 | 7 | |
| 4 | 8 | |
| 5 | 19 | |

**Step 3:** Press `Enter`. Excel will display `TRUE` in B1 since 5 is an odd number.

| | A | B |
|---|---|---|
| 1 | 5 | TRUE |
| 2 | 12 | |
| 3 | 7 | |
| 4 | 8 | |
| 5 | 19 | |
| 6 | | |

**Step 4:** Drag the fill handle (a small square at the bottom-right corner of the cell) down from B1 to B5 to apply the `ISODD` function to the rest of the numbers. The results will be:

B1: TRUE
B2: FALSE
B3: TRUE
B4: FALSE
B5: TRUE

| | A | B |
|---|---|---|
| 1 | 5 | TRUE |
| 2 | 12 | FALSE |
| 3 | 7 | TRUE |
| 4 | 8 | FALSE |
| 5 | 19 | TRUE |

This indicates that the numbers 5, 7, and 19 in the list are odd.

# Function #3 - AVERAGE

The `AVERAGE` function in Excel calculates the average (arithmetic mean) of a set of numbers. The average is the sum of the numbers divided by the count of numbers. This function is invaluable in a multitude of scenarios:

**1. Financial Analysis:** To determine the average sales, revenue, or any other financial metric over a period.
**2. Academic Grading:** To compute the average score of students.
**3. Scientific Research:** To find the mean value of a dataset.
**4. Business Metrics:** To understand average customer reviews, average product ratings, etc.

---

## Step-by-Step Guide

Step 1: Open your Excel workbook and navigate to the worksheet where you want to use the `AVERAGE` function.

Step 2: Click on the cell where you want the average result to appear.

Step 3: Enter the `AVERAGE` function. The syntax for the function is:

---

**=AVERAGE(number1, [number2], ...)**

---

- `number1, number2, ...` are the numbers, cell references, or ranges for which you want the average.

> ➤ **Depending on your country, the ' , ' must be replaced by ' ; '**

**Step 4:** After entering the required numbers or range, press `Enter`. Excel will display the average of the numbers in the selected cell.

---

## Example:

**Downloadable example:**
https://tinyurl.com/102-excel-functions

Imagine you're a teacher and you want to calculate the average score of a student's five tests.

**Step 1:** Enter the test scores in column A, starting from A1. For instance:

A1: 85

A2: 90

A3: 78

A4: 88

A5: 92

| | A |
|---|---|
| 1 | 85 |
| 2 | 90 |
| 3 | 78 |
| 4 | 88 |
| 5 | 92 |

**Step 2:** In cell B1, enter the `AVERAGE` function to calculate the average score of the five tests:

=AVERAGE(A1:A5)

| | A | B | C |
|---|---|---|---|
| 1 | 85 | =AVERAGE(A1:A5) | |
| 2 | 90 | | |
| 3 | 78 | | |
| 4 | 88 | | |
| 5 | 92 | | |

**Step 3:** Press `Enter`. Excel will display the average score in B1. For the given scores, the average will be `86.6`.

| | A | B |
|---|---|---|
| 1 | 85 | 86,6 |
| 2 | 90 | |
| 3 | 78 | |
| 4 | 88 | |
| 5 | 92 | |

**Note:** The `AVERAGE` function automatically ignores empty cells and cells containing text. However, it will consider cells with a value of zero in its calculations.

# Function #4 - INDEX

The `INDEX` function in Excel returns the value of a cell within a specific row and column of a range. It's a cornerstone function for advanced Excel users because of its versatility and the following benefits:

**1. Lookup Capabilities:** Unlike VLOOKUP or HLOOKUP, `INDEX` can return a value from both rows and columns, making it more flexible.

**2. Array Formulas:** It can be used in array formulas to return arrays, not just single values.

**3. Combination with MATCH:** When combined with the `MATCH` function, it can replicate or even surpass the functionality of VLOOKUP, without the limitation of always searching in the first column.

**4. Dynamic Range Selection:** Useful for creating dynamic named ranges or charts.

---

## Step-by-Step Guide

**Step 1:** Open your Excel workbook and navigate to the worksheet where you want to use the `INDEX` function.

**Step 2:** Click on the cell where you want the result to appear.

**Step 3:** Enter the `INDEX` function. The syntax for the function is:

> **=INDEX(array, row_num, [column_num])**

- `array` is the range of cells or table array.
- `row_num` is the row number in the array from which to return a value. If omitted, `column_num` is required.
- `column_num` (optional) is the column number from which to return a value.

> ➢ **Depending on your country, the ' , ' must be replaced by ' ; '**

**Step 4:** After entering the required parameters, press `Enter`. Excel will display the value from the specified cell in the array.

---

# Example

**Downloadable example:**
https://tinyurl.com/102-excel-functions

Imagine you have a table of students and their scores in different subjects. You want to find out the score of the third student in the subject "Math."

Data:

|   | A | B | C | D |
|---|------|------|-----|-----|
| 1 | Name | Math | Sci | Eng |
| 2 | John | 85 | 90 | 88 |
| 3 | Amy | 78 | 82 | 91 |
| 4 | Mark | 92 | 88 | 85 |

|   | A | B | C | D |
|---|------|------|-----|-----|
| 1 | Name | Math | Sci | Eng |
| 2 | John | 85 | 90 | 88 |
| 3 | Amy | 78 | 82 | 91 |
| 4 | Mark | 92 | 88 | 85 |

**Step 1:** Navigate to an empty cell where you want the result.

**Step 2:** Enter the `INDEX` function to find Mark's Math score:

=INDEX(B2:B4, 3)

|   | A | B | C | D | E |
|---|------|------|-----|-----|-------------------|
| 1 | Name | Math | Sci | Eng | =INDEX(B2:B4; 3) |
| 2 | John | 85 | 90 | 88 | |
| 3 | Amy | 78 | 82 | 91 | |
| 4 | Mark | 92 | 88 | 85 | |

**Step 3:** Press `Enter`. Excel will display the result `92` in the selected cell, which is Mark's score in Math.

| | A | B | C | D | E |
|---|---|---|---|---|---|
| 1 | Name | Math | Sci | Eng | 92 |
| 2 | John | 85 | 90 | 88 | |
| 3 | Amy | 78 | 82 | 91 | |
| 4 | Mark | 92 | 88 | 85 | |

---

**Advanced Tip:** Combining `INDEX` with `MATCH` can allow you to look up a value based on both row and column criteria. For instance, to find the score of a student named "Amy" in "Sci", you'd use:

=INDEX(B2:D4, MATCH("Amy", A2:A4, 0), MATCH("Sci",B1:D1, 0))

---

# Function #5 - MAX

The `MAX` function in Excel returns the largest value from a set of numbers. It's a simple yet powerful function with a range of applications:

**1. Data Analysis:** Quickly identify the highest value in a dataset.
**2. Financial Planning:** Determine the highest sales, revenue, or any other financial metric in a given period.
**3. Performance Tracking:** Identify the best performance or highest score.
**4. Inventory Management:** Find out the maximum stock level of a product.

---

**Step-by-Step Guide**

**Step 1:** Open your Excel workbook and navigate to the worksheet where you want to use the `MAX` function.

**Step 2:** Click on the cell where you want the maximum result to appear.

**Step 3:** Enter the `MAX` function. The syntax for the function is:

---

| =MAX(number1, [number2], ...) |
| --- |

- `number1, number2, ...` are the numbers, cell references, or ranges from which you want to find the maximum value.

> ➤ **Depending on your country, the ' , ' must be replaced by ' ; '**

**Step 4:** After entering the required numbers or range, press `Enter`. Excel will display the largest of the numbers in the selected cell.

---

# Example

**Downloadable example:**
https://tinyurl.com/102-excel-functions

Imagine you're a teacher and you want to determine the highest score from a set of test scores.

**Data:**
A1: Student Names
B1: Test Scores
A2: John
B2: 85

A3: Amy

B3: 92

A4: Mark

B4: 88

A5: Sarah

B5: 90

| | A | B |
|---|---|---|
| 1 | Student Names | Test Scores |
| 2 | John | 85 |
| 3 | Amy | 92 |
| 4 | Mark | 88 |
| 5 | Sarah | 90 |

**Step 1:** Navigate to an empty cell, say C1, where you want the result.

**Step 2:** Enter the `MAX` function to find the highest test score:

=MAX(B2:B5)

| | A | B | C |
|---|---|---|---|
| 1 | Student Names | Test Scores | =MAX(B2:B5) |
| 2 | John | 85 | |
| 3 | Amy | 92 | |
| 4 | Mark | 88 | |
| 5 | Sarah | 90 | |

**Step 3:** Press `Enter`. Excel will display the result `92` in C1, indicating that the highest score among the students is 92.

| | A | B | C |
|---|---|---|---|
| 1 | Student Names | Test Scores | 92 |
| 2 | John | 85 | |
| 3 | Amy | 92 | |
| 4 | Mark | 88 | |
| 5 | Sarah | 90 | |

**Note:** The `MAX` function will ignore empty cells, text, and logical values. However, if you want to include logical values (TRUE and FALSE) in the evaluation, you can use the `MAXA` function.

# Function #6 - TODAY

The `TODAY` function in Excel returns the current date. It provides the date in the format of the system's current date setting, updating automatically each time the worksheet is recalculated or opened. Here are some of its benefits:

**1. Dynamic Date Entry:** Instead of manually entering the current date, you can use `TODAY` to automatically populate and update it.

**2. Financial Analysis:** Calculate age of receivables, days until maturity, or any other metric that relies on the current date.

**3. Project Management:** Determine the number of days since a project started or days remaining until a project's deadline.

**4. Automated Reporting:** Ensure reports always reflect the current date without manual updates.

---

**Step-by-Step Guide**

**Step 1:** Open your Excel workbook and navigate to the worksheet where you want to use the `TODAY` function.

**Step 2:** Click on the cell where you want the current date to appear.

**Step 3:** Enter the `TODAY` function. The syntax for the function is simple:

---

**=TODAY()**

---

Note: The function doesn't require any arguments.

**Step 4:** Press `Enter`. Excel will display the current date in the selected cell.

---

**Example**

**Downloadable example:**
https://tinyurl.com/102-excel-functions

Imagine you're managing a library. You want to automatically record the date when a book is borrowed and calculate the due date, which is 14 days from the borrowing date.

**Step 1:** In cell A1, type "Borrow Date" and in cell B1, type "Due Date".

| ◢ | A | B |
|---|---|---|
| 1 | Borrow Date | Due Date |
| 2 | | |
| 3 | | |

**Step 2:** Click on cell A2 and enter the `TODAY` function:

=TODAY()

| ◢ | A | B |
|---|---|---|
| 1 | Borrow Date | Due Date |
| 2 | =TODAY() | |

**Step 3:** Press `Enter`. Excel will display the current date in A2.

| ◢ | A | B |
|---|---|---|
| 1 | Borrow Date | Due Date |
| 2 | 22/08/2023 | |

**Step 4:** In cell B2, calculate the due date by adding 14 days to the borrow date:

=A2 + 14

| ◢ | A | B |
|---|---|---|
| 1 | Borrow Date | Due Date |
| 2 | 22/08/2023 | =A2 + 14 |

28

**Step 5:** Press `Enter`. Excel will display the due date in B2, which will be 14 days from the current date.

| | A | B |
|---|---|---|
| 1 | Borrow Date | Due Date |
| 2 | 22/08/2023 | 05/09/2023 |

**Advanced Tip:** If you want the date to remain static and not update every day, you can manually enter the current date using the shortcut `Ctrl + ,` (semicolon). This will input the current date as a static value, not a dynamic one like the `TODAY` function.

# Function #7 - EOMONTH

The `EOMONTH` function in Excel returns the last day of the month that is a specified number of months before or after a given date. This function is particularly beneficial in various scenarios:

**1. Financial Planning:** Calculating maturity dates or end-of-month closing dates.

**2. Accounting:** Determining the last day of the month for monthly financial reconciliations.

**3. Inventory Management:** Setting end-of-month stocktaking or review dates.

**4. Project Management:** Estimating project end dates based on monthly cycles.

---

## Step-by-Step Guide

**Step 1:** Open your Excel workbook and navigate to the worksheet where you want to use the `EOMONTH` function.

**Step 2:** Click on the cell where you want the result to appear.

**Step 3:** Enter the `EOMONTH` function. The syntax for the function is:

---

## =EOMONTH(start_date, months)

---

- `start_date` is the starting date.
- `months` is the number of months before (negative value) or after (positive value) the start_date.

> ➢ **Depending on your country, the ' , ' must be replaced by ' ; '**

**Step 4:** After entering the required parameters, press `Enter`. Excel will display the date of the last day of the specified month in the selected cell.

---

## Example

**Downloadable example:**
https://tinyurl.com/102-excel-functions

Imagine you're a financial planner. You want to determine the end date of a 6-month investment plan that starts on January 15, 2023.

**Step 1:** In cell A1, type "Start Date" and enter the date "15-Jan-2023" in cell A2.

| | A |
|---|---|
| 1 | Start Date |
| 2 | 15/01/2023 |

**Step 2:** In cell B1, type "End Date".

| | A | B |
|---|---|---|
| 1 | Start Date | End Date |
| 2 | 15/01/2023 | |

**Step 3:** Click on cell B2 and enter the `EOMONTH` function to calculate the end date of the investment:

=EOMONTH(A2, 6)

| | A | B |
|---|---|---|
| 1 | Start Date | End Date |
| 2 | 15/01/2023 | =EOMONTH(A2; 6) |

**Step 4:** Press `Enter`. Excel will display the result `31-Jul-2023` in B2, indicating that the investment plan will end on July 31, 2023.

| | A | B |
|---|---|---|
| 1 | Start Date | End Date |
| 2 | 15/01/2023 | 31/07/2023 |

**Note:** The `EOMONTH` function can also be used to get the first day of a month by adding one day to the result of `EOMONTH` with a `-1` month argument. For example, to get the first day of the next month:

= EOMONTH(start_date, 0) + 1

# Function #8 - AVERAGEIFS

The `AVERAGEIFS` function calculates the average of numbers in a range that meet multiple specified criteria. It's an extension of the `AVERAGEIF` function, which works with a single criterion. Here are some of its benefits:

**1. Data Analysis:** Compute averages for specific subsets of data without creating separate tables or filters.

**2. Financial Analysis:** Determine the average sales of a particular product in a specific region or during a certain month.

**3. Academic Grading:** Calculate the average score of students who meet certain criteria, such as a specific major or year.

**4. Business Metrics:** Understand average customer reviews or product ratings based on multiple conditions.

---

### Step-by-Step Guide

**Step 1:** Open your Excel workbook and navigate to the worksheet where you want to use the `AVERAGEIFS` function.

**Step 2:** Click on the cell where you want the average result to appear.

**Step 3:** Enter the `AVERAGEIFS` function. The syntax for the function is:

> **=AVERAGEIFS(average_range, criteria_range1, criteria1, [criteria_range2, criteria2], ...)**

- `average_range` is the range of cells containing the numbers to be averaged.
- `criteria_range1` is the range of cells to be evaluated by `criteria1`.
- `criteria1` is the condition to be applied to `criteria_range1`.
- Additional criteria ranges and criteria can be added as needed.

> ➢ **Depending on your country, the ' , ' must be replaced by ' ; '**

**Step 4:** After entering the required ranges and criteria, press `Enter`. Excel will display the average of the numbers that meet all the specified criteria in the selected cell.

---

**Example**

**Downloadable example:**
https://tinyurl.com/102-excel-functions

Imagine you're a school administrator. You have a table of student grades and you want to determine the average score of 10th-grade students in the subject "Math."

**Data:**

| | A | B | C |
|---|---|---|---|
| 1 | Grade | Name | Math Score |
| 2 | 10 | John | 85 |
| 3 | 9 | Amy | 78 |
| 4 | 10 | Mark | 92 |
| 5 | 9 | Sarah | 88 |
| 6 | 10 | Mike | 89 |

| | A | B | C |
|---|---|---|---|
| 1 | Grade | Name | Math Score |
| 2 | 10 | John | 85 |
| 3 | 9 | Amy | 78 |
| 4 | 10 | Mark | 92 |
| 5 | 9 | Sarah | 88 |
| 6 | 10 | Mike | 89 |

**Step 1:** Navigate to an empty cell, say D1, where you want the result.

**Step 2:** Enter the `AVERAGEIFS` function to find the average Math score of 10th-grade students:

=AVERAGEIFS(C2:C6, A2:A6, 10)

| | A | B | C | D |
|---|---|---|---|---|
| | | | | =AVERAGEIFS(C2:C6; A2:A6; 10) |
| 1 | Grade | Name | Math Score | |
| 2 | 10 | John | 85 | |
| 3 | 9 | Amy | 78 | |
| 4 | 10 | Mark | 92 | |
| 5 | 9 | Sarah | 88 | |
| 6 | 10 | Mike | 89 | |

**Step 3:** Press `Enter`. Excel will display the result `88.67` in D1, indicating that the average Math score for 10th-grade students is approximately 88.67.

| | A | B | C | D |
|---|---|---|---|---|
| 1 | Grade | Name | Math Score | 88,66666667 |
| 2 | 10 | John | 85 | |
| 3 | 9 | Amy | 78 | |
| 4 | 10 | Mark | 92 | |
| 5 | 9 | Sarah | 88 | |
| 6 | 10 | Mike | 89 | |

---

**Advanced Tip:** You can add more criteria to further filter the data. For instance, if you wanted the average score of 10th-grade students who scored above 80 in Math, you'd use:

=AVERAGEIFS(C2:C6, A2:A6, 10, C2:C6, ">80")

---

# Function #9 - FLOOR

The `FLOOR` function in Excel is designed to round numbers down, towards zero, to the nearest multiple of a given factor. This function can be particularly beneficial in various scenarios, such as:

**1. Financial Planning:** When you want to avoid fractions of cents in financial calculations.
**2. Inventory Management:** To round down order quantities to the nearest box or package size.
**3. Time Management:** To round down time entries to the nearest quarter or half-hour.
**4. Manufacturing:** To determine the number of materials needed, rounded down to whole units.

---

## Step-by-Step Guide

**Step 1:** Open your Excel workbook and navigate to the worksheet where you want to use the `FLOOR` function.

**Step 2:** Click on the cell where you want the rounded result to appear.

**Step 3:** Enter the `FLOOR` function. The syntax for the function is:

| =FLOOR(number, significance) |
| --- |

- `number` is the value you want to round down.
- `significance` is the multiple to which you want to round down.

> ➢ **Depending on your country, the ' , ' must be replaced by ' ; '**

**Step 4:** After entering the required values, press `Enter`. Excel will display the rounded number in the selected cell.

---

## Example

**Downloadable example:**
https://tinyurl.com/102-excel-functions

Imagine you're a manufacturer who produces widgets. Each box can contain 8 widgets. You've received an order for 37 widgets. You want to determine how many full boxes you can create with this order.

**Step 1:** Enter the number of widgets ordered in cell A1 (37 in this case).

| | A |
|---|---|
| 1 | 37 |

**Step 2:** In cell B1, enter the number of widgets per box (8 in this case).

| | A | B |
|---|---|---|
| 1 | 37 | 8 |

**Step 3:** In cell C1, enter the `FLOOR` function to determine the number of full boxes you can create:

=FLOOR(A1/B1, 1)

| | A | B | C |
|---|---|---|---|
| 1 | 37 | 8 | =FLOOR(A1/B1; 1) |
| 2 | | | |

**Step 4:** Press `Enter`. Excel will display the result `4` in cell C1. This means you can create 4 full boxes with the 37 widgets, with 5 widgets remaining.

| | A | B | C |
|---|---|---|---|
| 1 | 37 | 8 | 4 |

**Note:** The `FLOOR` function always rounds towards zero. If you're working with negative numbers, it will round them down (towards zero), making them less negative.

# Function #10 - PROPER

The `PROPER` function in Excel converts a text string to proper case, meaning the first letter of each word is capitalized, and all other letters are in lowercase. This function is especially beneficial in various scenarios:

**1. Data Cleaning:** Standardizing names, titles, or any text data imported from external sources.

**2. Database Management:** Ensuring consistency in records, especially when dealing with user-submitted data.

**3. Report Presentation:** Making sure titles and names are presented in a standardized format.

**4. Form Responses:** Automatically formatting form responses for better readability.

---

## Step-by-Step Guide

**Step 1:** Open your Excel workbook and navigate to the worksheet where you want to use the `PROPER` function.

**Step 2:** Click on the cell where you want the properly formatted text to appear.

**Step 3:** Enter the `PROPER` function. The syntax for the function is:

---

## =PROPER(text)

---

- `text` is the text string or cell reference you want to convert to proper case.

**Step 4:** After entering the required text or cell reference, press `Enter`. Excel will display the text in proper case in the selected cell.

---

### Example

Imagine you've imported a list of names from an external database, but they're all in uppercase. You want to convert them to proper case for better presentation.

**Downloadable example:**
https://tinyurl.com/102-excel-functions

**Data:**

A1: JOHN DOE
A2: JANE SMITH
A3: ALICE JOHNSON

| | A |
|---|---|
| 1 | JOHN DOE |
| 2 | JANE SMITH |
| 3 | ALICE JOHNSON |

**Step 1:** Click on cell B1, where you want the properly formatted name to appear.

**Step 2:** Enter the `PROPER` function to convert the name in A1 to proper case:

=PROPER(A1)

| | A | B |
|---|---|---|
| 1 | JOHN DOE | =PROPER(A1) |
| 2 | JANE SMITH | |
| 3 | ALICE JOHNSON | |

**Step 3:** Press `Enter`. Excel will display the result `John Doe` in B1.

| | A | B |
|---|---|---|
| 1 | JOHN DOE | John Doe |
| 2 | JANE SMITH | |
| 3 | ALICE JOHNSON | |

**Step 4:** Drag the fill handle (a small square at the bottom-right corner of the cell) down from B1 to B3 to apply the `PROPER` function to the rest of the names. The results will be:

B1: John Doe

B2: Jane Smith

B3: Alice Johnson

| | A | B |
|---|---|---|
| 1 | JOHN DOE | John Doe |
| 2 | JANE SMITH | Jane Smith |
| 3 | ALICE JOHNSON | Alice Johnson |

> **Note:** The `PROPER` function only capitalizes the first letter of each word. If a name has an apostrophe, like "O'CONNOR", it will be converted to "O'Connor", which is the desired format.

# Function #11 - COUNTA

The `COUNTA` function in Excel counts the number of cells in a range that are not empty. This means it counts cells containing numbers, text, logical values, errors, and other types of information. Here are some of its benefits:

**1. Data Analysis:** Quickly determine the number of entries in a list or dataset.
**2. Database Management:** Check the number of records or entries in a column or row.
**3. Form Responses:** Count the number of responses or entries in a survey or form.
**4. Error Checking:** Identify columns or rows that might be missing data by comparing expected counts to actual counts.

---

## Step-by-Step Guide

**Step 1:** Open your Excel workbook and navigate to the worksheet where you want to use the `COUNTA` function.

**Step 2:** Click on the cell where you want the count result to appear.

**Step 3:** Enter the `COUNTA` function. The syntax for the function is:

| |
|---|
| **=COUNTA(range)** |

- `range` is the range of cells you want to count non-empty cells from.

**Step 4:** After entering the desired range, press `Enter`. Excel will display the count of non-empty cells in the selected range.

---

**Example**

**Downloadable example:**
https://tinyurl.com/102-excel-functions

Imagine you're managing a registration desk for an event. You have a list of attendees, but some cells might be empty due to no-shows or last-minute cancellations. You want to determine the actual number of attendees.

**Data:**

A1: Attendees
A2: John Doe
A3: Jane Smith

A4: [empty cell]
A5: Alice Johnson
A6: [empty cell]
A7: Mark Brown

| | A |
|---|---|
| 1 | Attendees |
| 2 | John Doe |
| 3 | Jane Smith |
| 4 | |
| 5 | Alice Johnson |
| 6 | |
| 7 | Mark Brown |

**Step 1:** Click on cell B1, where you want the count of attendees to appear.

**Step 2:** Enter the `COUNTA` function to count the number of attendees from A2 to A7:

=COUNTA(A2:A7)

| | A | B |
|---|---|---|
| 1 | Attendees | =COUNTA(A2:A7) |
| 2 | John Doe | |
| 3 | Jane Smith | |
| 4 | | |
| 5 | Alice Johnson | |
| 6 | | |
| 7 | Mark Brown | |

**Step 3:** Press `Enter`. Excel will display the result `4` in B1, indicating that there are four attendees in the list.

| ◢ | A | B |
|---|---|---|
| 1 | Attendees | 4 |
| 2 | John Doe | |
| 3 | Jane Smith | |
| 4 | | |
| 5 | Alice Johnson | |
| 6 | | |
| 7 | Mark Brown | |

**Note:** The `COUNTA` function counts all types of data except for empty cells. If you only want to count cells with numbers, you'd use the `COUNT` function. If you want to count cells based on specific criteria, you'd use the `COUNTIF` or `COUNTIFS` functions.

# Function #12 - RIGHT

The `RIGHT` function in Excel is used to extract a specified number of characters from the end (right side) of a text string. This function is particularly beneficial in various scenarios:

**1. Data Cleaning:** Extracting specific parts of data from larger text strings.

**2. Database Management:** Retrieving the last few characters of product codes, serial numbers, or any other alphanumeric identifiers.

**3. Financial Analysis:** Extracting the cents portion from a full currency value.

**4. Text Analysis:** Parsing data based on known structures, like extracting domain extensions from URLs.

---

### Step-by-Step Guide

**Step 1:** Open your Excel workbook and navigate to the worksheet where you want to use the `RIGHT` function.

**Step 2:** Click on the cell where you want the extracted text to appear.

**Step 3:** Enter the `RIGHT` function. The syntax for the function is:

---

**=RIGHT(text, [num_chars])**

---

- `text` is the text string or cell reference from which you want to extract characters.
- `num_chars` (optional) specifies the number of characters you want to extract. If omitted, it defaults to 1.

> ➤ **Depending on your country, the ' , ' must be replaced by ' ; '**

**Step 4:** After entering the required text and number of characters, press `Enter`. Excel will display the extracted characters in the selected cell.

---

**Example**

**Downloadable example:**
https://tinyurl.com/102-excel-functions

Imagine you're managing a list of product codes where the last three characters represent the product's category. You want to extract these category codes for analysis.

**Data:**

A1: Product Code
A2: XYZ-001-ABC
A3: XYZ-002-DEF
A4: XYZ-003-GHI

| | A |
|---|---|
| 1 | Product Code |
| 2 | XYZ-001-ABC |
| 3 | XYZ-002-DEF |
| 4 | XYZ-003-GHI |

**Step 1:** Click on cell B1 and type "Category Code" as the header.

**Step 2:** In cell B2, enter the `RIGHT` function to extract the last three characters from the product code in A2:

=RIGHT(A2, 3)

| | A | B |
|---|---|---|
| 1 | Product Code | Category Code |
| 2 | XYZ-001-ABC | =RIGHT(A2; 3) |
| 3 | XYZ-002-DEF | |
| 4 | XYZ-003-GHI | |

**Step 3:** Press `Enter`. Excel will display the result `ABC` in B2.

|   | A | B |
|---|---|---|
| 1 | Product Code | Category Code |
| 2 | XYZ-001-ABC | ABC |
| 3 | XYZ-002-DEF | |
| 4 | XYZ-003-GHI | |

**Step 4:** Drag the fill handle (a small square at the bottom-right corner of the cell) down from B2 to B4 to apply the `RIGHT` function to the rest of the product codes. The results will be:

B2: ABC
B3: DEF
B4: GHI

|   | A | B |
|---|---|---|
| 1 | Product Code | Category Code |
| 2 | XYZ-001-ABC | ABC |
| 3 | XYZ-002-DEF | DEF |
| 4 | XYZ-003-GHI | GHI |

> **Note:** The `RIGHT` function is often used in combination with other text functions like `LEN` to create more dynamic text manipulations based on the length of the string.

# Function #13 - RANK

The `RANK` function in Excel returns the rank of a number within a set of numbers. This function is particularly beneficial in various scenarios:

1. **Data Analysis:** Determine the standing of a specific data point within a dataset.
2. **Sales Performance:** Rank sales representatives based on their sales figures.
3. **Academic Grading:** Rank students based on their scores or grades.
4. **Sports Statistics:** Rank teams or players based on performance metrics.

---

## Step-by-Step Guide

**Step 1:** Open your Excel workbook and navigate to the worksheet where you want to use the `RANK` function.

**Step 2:** Click on the cell where you want the rank result to appear.

**Step 3:** Enter the `RANK` function. The syntax for the function is:

| =RANK(number, ref, [order]) |
| --- |

- `number` is the number you want to find the rank for.
- `ref` is an array of, or reference to, a list of numbers.
- `order` (optional) is a number specifying how to rank the number. If omitted or set to 0, the function will rank the largest number as 1. If set to any non-zero value, it will rank the smallest number as 1.

> ➢ **Depending on your country, the ' , ' must be replaced by ' ; '**

**Step 4:** After entering the required values and range, press `Enter`. Excel will display the rank of the number in the selected cell.

---

**Example**

**Downloadable example:**
https://tinyurl.com/102-excel-functions

**Scenario:** Imagine you're a teacher who wants to rank students based on their test scores.

**Data:**

A1: Student Name   B1: Score
A2: John          B2: 85
A3: Amy           B3: 92
A4: Mark          B4: 88
A5: Sarah         B5: 90

| | A | B |
|---|---|---|
| 1 | Student Name | Score |
| 2 | John | 85 |
| 3 | Amy | 92 |
| 4 | Mark | 88 |
| 5 | Sarah | 90 |

**Step 1:** Click on cell C1 and type "Rank" as the header.

| | A | B | C |
|---|---|---|---|
| 1 | Student Name | Score | Rank |
| 2 | John | 85 | |
| 3 | Amy | 92 | |
| 4 | Mark | 88 | |
| 5 | Sarah | 90 | |

**Step 2:** In cell C2, enter the `RANK` function to rank John's score:

=RANK(B2, B2:B5)

| | A | B | C |
|---|---|---|---|
| 1 | Student Name | Score | Rank |
| 2 | John | 85 | =RANK(B2; B2:B5) |
| 3 | Amy | 92 | |
| 4 | Mark | 88 | |
| 5 | Sarah | 90 | |

**Step 3:** Press `Enter`. Excel will display the result `4` in C2, indicating that John has the 4th highest score.

| | A | B | C |
|---|---|---|---|
| 1 | Student Name | Score | Rank |
| 2 | John | 85 | 4 |
| 3 | Amy | 92 | |
| 4 | Mark | 88 | |
| 5 | Sarah | 90 | |

**Step 4:** Change the formula for each of the other rows by replacing B2 with B3 for Amy

| | A | B | C |
|---|---|---|---|
| 1 | Student Name | Score | Rank |
| 2 | John | 85 | 4 |
| 3 | Amy | 92 | =RANK(B3; B2:B5) |
| 4 | Mark | 88 | 3 |
| 5 | Sarah | 90 | 2 |

The results will be:

C2: 4

C3: 1

C4: 3

C5: 2

| ▲ | A | B | C |
|---|---|---|---|
| 1 | Student Name | Score | Rank |
| 2 | John | 85 | 4 |
| 3 | Amy | 92 | 1 |
| 4 | Mark | 88 | 3 |
| 5 | Sarah | 90 | 2 |

**Note:** In newer versions of Excel, the `RANK` function has been replaced with two functions: `RANK.EQ` (which behaves the same as `RANK`) and `RANK.AVG` (which averages ranks for tied numbers). However, `RANK` is still available for compatibility with older versions.

# Function #14 - MROUND

The `MROUND` function in Excel rounds a number up or down to the nearest specified multiple. This function is especially beneficial in various scenarios:

**1. Financial Planning:** Rounding amounts to the nearest dollar, 5 dollars, 10 dollars, etc.

**2. Inventory Management:** Rounding quantities to the nearest package or box size.

**3. Time Management:** Rounding time entries to the nearest quarter or half-hour.

**4. Manufacturing:** Rounding measurements to standard unit sizes.

---

## Step-by-Step Guide

**Step 1:** Open your Excel workbook and navigate to the worksheet where you want to use the `MROUND` function.

**Step 2:** Click on the cell where you want the rounded result to appear.

**Step 3:** Enter the `MROUND` function. The syntax for the function is:

---

**=MROUND(number, multiple)**

---

- `number` is the value you want to round.
- `multiple` is the multiple to which you want to round the number.

> ➢ **Depending on your country, the ' , ' must be replaced by ' ; '**

**Step 4:** After entering the desired number and multiple, press `Enter`. Excel will display the rounded number in the selected cell.

---

## Example

**Downloadable example:**
https://tinyurl.com/102-excel-functions

Imagine you're a warehouse manager. You have products that are packed in boxes of 8. You've received an order for 37 units of a product. You want to determine how many full boxes you'll need, rounding up to ensure all products are included.

**Step 1:** Enter the number of units ordered in cell A1 (37 in this case).

| | A |
|---|---|
| 1 | 37 |

**Step 2:** In cell B1, enter the number of units per box (8 in this case).

| | A | B |
|---|---|---|
| 1 | 37 | 8 |

**Step 3:** In cell C1, enter the `MROUND` function to determine the total units you'll need when rounded to the nearest box:

=MROUND(A1, B1)

| | A | B | C |
|---|---|---|---|
| 1 | 37 | 8 | =MROUND(A1; B1) |

**Step 4:** Press `Enter`. Excel will display the result `40` in C1. This means you'll need enough boxes to accommodate 40 units to fulfill the order of 37, ensuring all products are packed.

| | A | B | C |
|---|---|---|---|
| 1 | 37 | 8 | 40 |

> **Note:** If the number is exactly halfway between two multiples, `MROUND` will round away from zero. For example, `MROUND(5, 10)` will round to 10.

# Function #15 - SUBSTITUTE

The `SUBSTITUTE` function in Excel replaces existing text with new text in a text string. It's particularly useful in a variety of scenarios:

**1. Data Cleaning:** Correcting typos or standardizing terminology in datasets.
**2. Text Transformation:** Modifying URLs, file paths, or any structured text data.
**3. Data Analysis:** Converting certain text values to others for better categorization or analysis.
**4. Formatting:** Adjusting text data to fit a desired format or template.

---

**Step-by-Step Guide**

**Step 1:** Open your Excel workbook and navigate to the worksheet where you want to use the `SUBSTITUTE` function.

**Step 2:** Click on the cell where you want the modified text to appear.

**Step 3:** Enter the `SUBSTITUTE` function. The syntax for the function is:

| =SUBSTITUTE(text, old_text, new_text, [instance_num]) |
| --- |

- `text` is the original text string or cell reference.
- `old_text` is the text you want to replace.
- `new_text` is the text you want to replace `old_text` with.
- `instance_num` (optional) specifies which occurrence of `old_text` you want to replace. If omitted, every occurrence is replaced.

> ➤ **Depending on your country, the ' , ' must be replaced by ' ; '**

**Step 4:** After entering the required parameters, press `Enter`. Excel will display the modified text in the selected cell.

---

**Example**

**Downloadable example:**
https://tinyurl.com/102-excel-functions

Imagine you're managing a list of product URLs for an online store. The domain of the store has recently changed from "oldstore.com" to "newstore.com", and you need to update the URLs.

**Data:**

A1: Product URL
A2: https://www.oldstore.com/product1
A3: https://www.oldstore.com/product2
A4: https://www.oldstore.com/product3

| | A |
|---|---|
| 1 | Product URL |
| 2 | https://www.oldstore.com/product1 |
| 3 | https://www.oldstore.com/product2 |
| 4 | https://www.oldstore.com/product3 |

**Step 1:** Click on cell B1 and type "Updated URL" as the header.

| | A | B |
|---|---|---|
| 1 | Product URL | Updated URL |
| 2 | https://www.oldstore.com/product1 | |
| 3 | https://www.oldstore.com/product2 | |
| 4 | https://www.oldstore.com/product3 | |

**Step 2:** In cell B2, enter the `SUBSTITUTE` function to update the domain in the URL:

=SUBSTITUTE(A2, "oldstore.com", "newstore.com")

| | A | B | C | D |
|---|---|---|---|---|
| 1 | Product URL | Updated URL | | |
| 2 | https://www.oldstore.com/product1 | =SUBSTITUTE(A2; "oldstore.com"; "newstore.com") | | |
| 3 | https://www.oldstore.com/product2 | | | |
| 4 | https://www.oldstore.com/product3 | | | |

**Step 3:** Press `Enter`. Excel will display the updated URL `https://www.newstore.com/product1` in B2.

| | A | B |
|---|---|---|
| 1 | Product URL | Updated URL |
| 2 | https://www.oldstore.com/product1 | https://www.newstore.com/product1 |
| 3 | https://www.oldstore.com/product2 | |
| 4 | https://www.oldstore.com/product3 | |

**Step 4:** Drag the fill handle (a small square at the bottom-right corner of the cell) down from B2 to B4 to apply the `SUBSTITUTE` function to the rest of the URLs. The results will be:

B2: https://www.newstore.com/product1
B3: https://www.newstore.com/product2
B4: https://www.newstore.com/product3

| | A | B |
|---|---|---|
| 1 | Product URL | Updated URL |
| 2 | https://www.oldstore.com/product1 | https://www.newstore.com/product1 |
| 3 | https://www.oldstore.com/product2 | https://www.newstore.com/product2 |
| 4 | https://www.oldstore.com/product3 | https://www.newstore.com/product3 |
| 5 | | |

**Advanced Tip:** If you only wanted to replace the first occurrence or a specific occurrence of a text string, you'd use the `instance_num` parameter. For example, if you had a text string "apple banana apple" and you only wanted to replace the first "apple" with "grape", you'd use:

=SUBSTITUTE("apple banana apple", "apple", "grape", 1)

The result would be "grape banana apple".

# Function #16 - DATE

The `DATE` function in Excel returns a serial number that represents a specific date. This function is especially beneficial in various scenarios:

**1. Data Analysis:** Constructing date values based on individual year, month, and day components.
**2. Financial Analysis:** Creating specific date milestones for financial modeling.
**3. Project Management:** Setting start or end dates based on given parameters.
**4. Event Planning:** Generating event dates based on certain criteria.

---

### Step-by-Step Guide

**Step 1:** Open your Excel workbook and navigate to the worksheet where you want to use the `DATE` function.

**Step 2:** Click on the cell where you want the date value to appear.

**Step 3:** Enter the `DATE` function. The syntax for the function is:

> **=DATE(year, month, day)**

- `year` is the year of the date.
- `month` is the month of the date.
- `day` is the day of the month.

> ➤ **Depending on your country, the ' , ' must be replaced by ' ; '**

**Step 4:** After entering the desired year, month, and day values, press `Enter`. Excel will display the date in the selected cell.

---

## Example

**Downloadable example:**
https://tinyurl.com/102-excel-functions

Imagine you're planning an event. You know the event will take place in 2023, during the 5th month (May), on the 15th day.

**Step 1:** Click on cell A1 where you want the event date to appear.

**Step 2:** Enter the `DATE` function with the given parameters:

=DATE(2023, 5, 15)

| | A |
|---|---|
| 1 | =DATE(2023; 5; 15) |
| 2 | |

**Step 3:** Press `Enter`. Excel will display the result `5/15/2023` in A1 (the format might vary based on your regional settings).

| | A |
|---|---|
| 1 | 15/05/2023 |
| 2 | |

**Advanced Tips:**

**1. Adding or Subtracting Dates:** You can add or subtract days, months, or years using the `DATE` function. For example, to get a date 15 days after the event, you'd use:

=DATE(2023, 5, 15) + 15

The result would be `5/30/2023`.

**2. Handling Invalid Dates:** If you provide an invalid day value, such as 32 (since no month has 32 days), Excel will roll over to the next month. For instance, `=DATE(2023, 5, 32)` would result in `6/1/2023`.

**3. Using with Other Functions:** The `DATE` function can be combined with other date functions like `YEAR`, `MONTH`, and `DAY` to extract and manipulate date components.

# Function #17 - ISEVEN

The `ISEVEN` function in Excel checks if a given number is even and returns `TRUE` if it is, and `FALSE` if it's not. This function is particularly beneficial in various scenarios:

**1. Data Analysis:** Filtering or categorizing data based on even or odd criteria.

2. Mathematical Studies: Evaluating sequences or sets of numbers.

3. Programming Logic: Implementing conditional logic based on evenness.

4. Financial Analysis: Applying specific conditions or formulas for even periods or intervals.

---

## Step-by-Step Guide

**Step 1:** Open your Excel workbook and navigate to the worksheet where you want to use the `ISEVEN` function.

**Step 2:** Click on the cell where you want the result (TRUE or FALSE) to appear.

**Step 3:** Enter the `ISEVEN` function. The syntax for the function is:

---

## =ISEVEN(number)

---

- `number` is the value you want to check.

**Step 4:** After entering the desired number or cell reference, press `Enter`. Excel will display `TRUE` if the number is even and `FALSE` if it's not.

---

### Example

**Downloadable example:**
https://tinyurl.com/102-excel-functions

Imagine you're a teacher creating a fun activity for students. You have a list of numbers, and you want to label which ones are even.

Data:

A1: Number   B1: Is Even?
A2: 5
A3: 12
A4: 7
A5: 8

| | A | B |
|---|---|---|
| 1 | Number | Is Even ? |
| 2 | 5 | |
| 3 | 12 | |
| 4 | 7 | |
| 5 | 8 | |

**Step 1:** Click on cell B2, where you want to check if the number in A2 is even.

**Step 2:** Enter the `ISEVEN` function referring to the number in A2:

=ISEVEN(A2)

| | A | B |
|---|---|---|
| 1 | Number | Is Even ? |
| 2 | 5 | =ISEVEN(A2) |
| 3 | 12 | |
| 4 | 7 | |
| 5 | 8 | |

**Step 3:** Press `Enter`. Excel will display the result `FALSE` in B2 since 5 is not an even number.

| | A | B |
|---|---|---|
| 1 | Number | Is Even ? |
| 2 | 5 | FALSE |
| 3 | 12 | |
| 4 | 7 | |
| 5 | 8 | |

**Step 4:** Drag the fill handle (a small square at the bottom-right corner of the cell) down from B2 to B5 to apply the `ISEVEN` function to the rest of the numbers. The results will be:

B2: FALSE

B3: TRUE

B4: FALSE

B5: TRUE

| | A | B |
|---|---|---|
| 1 | Number | Is Even ? |
| 2 | 5 | FALSE |
| 3 | 12 | TRUE |
| 4 | 7 | FALSE |
| 5 | 8 | TRUE |

**Note:** There's also an `ISODD` function in Excel that works similarly but checks for odd numbers.

I hope this tutorial provides a clear understanding of the `ISEVEN` function in Excel and its practical applications!

# Function #18 - YEARFRAC

The `YEARFRAC` function in Excel calculates the proportion of a year between two specified dates. This function is especially beneficial in various scenarios:

**1. Financial Analysis:** Calculating interest accrued over non-whole year periods in financial models.

**2. Project Management:** Determining the fraction of a year a project took or will take.

**3. Human Resources:** Calculating employee benefits or entitlements based on partial years of service.

**4. Academic Settings:** Determining the fraction of an academic year completed.

---

**Step-by-Step Guide**

**Step 1:** Open your Excel workbook and navigate to the worksheet where you want to use the `YEARFRAC` function.

**Step 2:** Click on the cell where you want the fractional year value to appear.

**Step 3:** Enter the `YEARFRAC` function. The syntax for the function is:

> ## =YEARFRAC(start_date, end_date, [basis])

- `start_date` is the start date.
- `end_date` is the end date.
- `basis` (optional) is the type of day count basis to use. If omitted, it defaults to 0. The options are:
  - 0: US (NASD) 30/360
  - 1: Actual/actual
  - 2: Actual/360
  - 3: Actual/365
  - 4: European 30/360

> ➢ **Depending on your country, the ' , ' must be replaced by ' ; '**

**Step 4:** After entering the required dates and choosing a basis (if needed), press `Enter`. Excel will display the fraction of the year between the two dates in the selected cell.

---

## Example

**Downloadable example:**
https://tinyurl.com/102-excel-functions

Imagine you're a financial analyst calculating the interest for a loan taken out on January 1, 2023, and repaid on October 15, 2023. You want to determine the fraction of the year the loan was outstanding.

Data:

A1: Start Date    B1: 1/1/2023
A2: End Date      B2: 10/15/2023

| | A | B |
|---|---|---|
| 1 | Start Date | 01/01/2023 |
| 2 | End Date | 15/10/2023 |

**Step 1:** Click on cell A3 and type "Year Fraction".

**Step 2:** In cell B3, enter the `YEARFRAC` function referring to the start and end dates:

=YEARFRAC(B1, B2)

| | A | B |
|---|---|---|
| 1 | Start Date | 01/01/2023 |
| 2 | End Date | 15/10/2023 |
| 3 | | =YEARFRAC(B1; B2) |

**Step 3:** Press `Enter`. Excel will display the result `0.7973` in B3, indicating the loan was outstanding for approximately 79.73% of the year.

| | A | B |
|---|---|---|
| 1 | Start Date | 01/01/2023 |
| 2 | End Date | 15/10/2023 |
| 3 | | 0,788888889 |

**Advanced Tip:** If you wanted to use a different day count basis, you'd include the `basis` parameter. For instance, for an Actual/365 basis, the formula would be:

=YEARFRAC(B1, B2, 3)

# Function #19 - NOT

The `NOT` function in Excel is used to reverse a logical value. If the given value is `TRUE`, the `NOT` function will return `FALSE`, and vice versa. This function is especially beneficial in various scenarios:

**1. Data Analysis:** Reversing the logic of filters or conditions.

**2. Conditional Formatting:** Applying formats based on the opposite of a given condition.

**3. Formulas and Functions:** Enhancing the flexibility of other logical functions like `IF`, `AND`, and `OR`.

**4. Programming Logic:** Implementing NOT logic gates or conditions in more complex Excel-based applications.

---

**Step-by-Step Guide**

**Step 1:** Open your Excel workbook and navigate to the worksheet where you want to use the `NOT` function.

**Step 2:** Click on the cell where you want the reversed logical value to appear.

**Step 3:** Enter the `NOT` function. The syntax for the function is:

---

**=NOT(logical)**

---

- `logical` is the logical value or expression you want to reverse.

**Step 4:** After entering the desired logical value or expression, press `Enter`. Excel will display the reversed logical value in the selected cell.

---

**Example**

**Downloadable example:**
https://tinyurl.com/102-excel-functions

Imagine you're a teacher who has a list of students and whether they've submitted their assignments. You want to create a list of students who haven't submitted their assignments.

Data:

A1: Student Name     B1: Submitted     C1: Not Submitted
A2: John          B2: TRUE

A3: Amy        B3: FALSE
A4: Mark       B4: TRUE
A5: Sarah      B5: FALSE

| | A | B | C |
|---|---|---|---|
| 1 | Student Name | Submitted | Not Submitted |
| 2 | John | TRUE | |
| 3 | Amy | FALSE | |
| 4 | Mark | TRUE | |
| 5 | Sarah | FALSE | |

**Step 1:** Click on cell C2, where you want to determine if John has not submitted his assignment.

**Step 2:** Enter the `NOT` function referring to the "Submitted" status for John:

=NOT(B2)

| | A | B | C |
|---|---|---|---|
| 1 | Student Name | Submitted | Not Submitted |
| 2 | John | TRUE | =NOT(B2) |
| 3 | Amy | FALSE | |
| 4 | Mark | TRUE | |
| 5 | Sarah | FALSE | |

**Step 3:** Press `Enter`. Excel will display the result `FALSE` in C2 since John has submitted his assignment.

| | A | B | C |
|---|---|---|---|
| 1 | Student Name | Submitted | Not Submitted |
| 2 | John | TRUE | FALSE |
| 3 | Amy | FALSE | |
| 4 | Mark | TRUE | |
| 5 | Sarah | FALSE | |

**Step 4:** Drag the fill handle (a small square at the bottom-right corner of the cell) down from C2 to C5 to apply the `NOT` function to the rest of the students. The results will be:

C2: FALSE
C3: TRUE
C4: FALSE
C5: TRUE

| | A | B | C |
|---|---|---|---|
| 1 | Student Name | Submitted | Not Submitted |
| 2 | John | TRUE | FALSE |
| 3 | Amy | FALSE | TRUE |
| 4 | Mark | TRUE | FALSE |
| 5 | Sarah | FALSE | TRUE |

This indicates that Amy and Sarah have not submitted their assignments.

**Note:** The `NOT` function is often used in combination with other logical functions to create more complex logical tests. For example, to test if a number is not equal to 5, you could use `=NOT(A1=5)`.

# Function #20 - MINIFS

The `MINIFS` function in Excel returns the smallest number in a range, based on multiple criteria. This function is especially beneficial in various scenarios:

**1. Data Analysis:** Finding the minimum value in a dataset that meets specific conditions.
**2. Inventory Management:** Identifying the lowest stock level for a particular category of items.
**3. Sales Analysis:** Determining the lowest sales figure for a specific product or region.
**4. Financial Analysis:** Extracting the minimum financial metric, like profit or revenue, for a particular segment or time period.

---

## Step-by-Step Guide

**Step 1:** Open your Excel workbook and navigate to the worksheet where you want to use the `MINIFS` function.

**Step 2:** Click on the cell where you want the minimum value to appear.

**Step 3:** Enter the `MINIFS` function. The syntax for the function is:

> =MINIFS(min_range, criteria_range1, criteria1, [criteria_range2, criteria2], ...)

- `min_range` is the range of numbers from which you want to find the minimum value.
- `criteria_range1` is the range of cells to be evaluated with the associated criteria.
- `criteria1` is the condition or criteria in the form of a number, expression, or text that defines which cells will be evaluated.
- Additional criteria ranges and criteria can be added as needed.

> ➢ **Depending on your country, the ' , ' must be replaced by ' ; '**

**Step 4:** After entering the required ranges and criteria, press `Enter`. Excel will display the minimum value that meets the criteria in the selected cell.

---

## Example

**Downloadable example:**
https://tinyurl.com/102-excel-functions

Imagine you're a store manager with sales data for various products. You want to find the lowest sales figure for a specific product category, "Electronics".

Data:

A1: Product Category   B1: Sales
A2: Electronics        B2: 500
A3: Clothing           B3: 300
A4: Electronics        B4: 450
A5: Home Goods         B5: 600
A6: Electronics        B6: 480

| | A | B |
|---|---|---|
| 1 | Product Category | Sales |
| 2 | Electronics | 500 |
| 3 | Clothing | 300 |
| 4 | Electronics | 450 |
| 5 | Home Goods | 600 |
| 6 | Electronics | 480 |

**Step 1:** Click on cell D1 and type "Lowest Electronics Sales".

| | A | B | C | D |
|---|---|---|---|---|
| 1 | Product Category | Sales | | Lowest Electronics Sales |
| 2 | Electronics | 500 | | |
| 3 | Clothing | 300 | | |
| 4 | Electronics | 450 | | |
| 5 | Home Goods | 600 | | |
| 6 | Electronics | 480 | | |
| 7 | | | | |

**Step 2:** In cell D2, enter the `MINIFS` function to find the lowest sales figure for the "Electronics" category:

=MINIFS(B2:B6, A2:A6, "Electronics")

**Step 3:** Press `Enter`. Excel will display the result `450` in D2, indicating the lowest sales figure for the "Electronics" category.

---

**Advanced Tip:** The `MINIFS` function can accommodate multiple criteria. For instance, if you wanted to find the lowest sales figure for "Electronics" in a specific region or during a particular month, you'd add more criteria ranges and criteria to the function.

---

# Function #21 - LOOKUP

The `LOOKUP` function in Excel is used to search for a value in a range or array and return a corresponding value from another range or array. This function is especially beneficial in various scenarios:

**1. Data Retrieval:** Extracting associated data based on a specific lookup value.
**2. Data Analysis:** Matching and comparing datasets.
**3. Sales and Inventory:** Finding product details based on product codes.
**4. Financial Analysis:** Retrieving financial metrics based on specific criteria.

While `VLOOKUP` and `HLOOKUP` are more commonly used and offer more specific lookup directions (vertical and horizontal, respectively), `LOOKUP` can be useful in situations where the direction is ambiguous or when working with sorted data.

### Step-by-Step Guide

**Step 1:** Open your Excel workbook and navigate to the worksheet where you want to use the `LOOKUP` function.

**Step 2:** Click on the cell where you want the retrieved data to appear.

**Step 3:** Enter the `LOOKUP` function. The syntax for the function is:

---

**=LOOKUP(lookup_value, lookup_vector, [result_vector])**

---

- `lookup_value` is the value you want to search for.
- `lookup_vector` is the range or array where you want to find the `lookup_value`.
- `result_vector` (optional) is the range or array from which you want to retrieve the data. If omitted, `lookup_vector` is used.

> ➢ **Depending on your country, the ' , ' must be replaced by ' ; '**

**Step 4:** After entering the required values and ranges, press `Enter`. Excel will display the corresponding value in the selected cell.

---

**Example**

**Downloadable example:**

https://tinyurl.com/102-excel-functions

Imagine you're a bookstore owner with a list of book codes and corresponding titles. A customer provides a book code, and you want to find the title of the book.

Data:

A1: Book Code  B1: Title
A2: BK001      B2: To Kill a Mockingbird
A3: BK002      B3: 1984
A4: BK003      B4: Pride and Prejudice
A5: BK004      B5: The Great Gatsby

| | A | B |
|---|---|---|
| 1 | Book Code | Title |
| 2 | BK001 | To Kill a Mockingbird |
| 3 | BK002 | 1984 |
| 4 | BK003 | Pride and Prejudice |
| 5 | BK004 | The Great Gatsby |

**Step 1:** In cell D1, type "Enter Book Code" and in D2, enter a book code, say "BK003".

| | A | B | C | D |
|---|---|---|---|---|
| 1 | Book Code | Title | | Enter Book Code |
| 2 | BK001 | To Kill a Mockingbird | | BK003 |
| 3 | BK002 | 1984 | | |
| 4 | BK003 | Pride and Prejudice | | |
| 5 | BK004 | The Great Gatsby | | |

**Step 2:** In cell E1, type "Book Title".

| | A | B | C | D | E |
|---|---|---|---|---|---|
| 1 | Book Code | Title | | Enter Book Code | Book Title |
| 2 | BK001 | To Kill a Mockingbird | | BK003 | |
| 3 | BK002 | 1984 | | | |
| 4 | BK003 | Pride and Prejudice | | | |
| 5 | BK004 | The Great Gatsby | | | |

**Step 3:** In cell E2, enter the `LOOKUP` function to find the book title for the code in D2:

=LOOKUP(D2, A2:A5, B2:B5)

| | A | B | C | D | E | F | G |
|---|---|---|---|---|---|---|---|
| 1 | Book Code | Title | | Enter Book Code | Book Title | | |
| 2 | BK001 | To Kill a Mockingbird | | BK003 | =LOOKUP(D2; A2:A5; B2:B5) | | |
| 3 | BK002 | 1984 | | | | | |
| 4 | BK003 | Pride and Prejudice | | | | | |
| 5 | BK004 | The Great Gatsby | | | | | |

**Step 4:** Press `Enter`. Excel will display the result "Pride and Prejudice" in E2, indicating the title for the book code "BK003".

| | A | B | C | D | E |
|---|---|---|---|---|---|
| 1 | Book Code | Title | | Enter Book Code | Book Title |
| 2 | BK001 | To Kill a Mockingbird | | BK003 | Pride and Prejudice |
| 3 | BK002 | 1984 | | | |
| 4 | BK003 | Pride and Prejudice | | | |
| 5 | BK004 | The Great Gatsby | | | |

**Note:** The `LOOKUP` function assumes that the `lookup_vector` is sorted in ascending order and will return the largest value that is less than or equal to the `lookup_value`. If the `lookup_value` is smaller than the smallest value in the `lookup_vector`, the function will return an error.

# Function #22 - LOWER

The `LOWER` function in Excel converts all characters in a text string to lowercase. This function is especially beneficial in various scenarios:

**1. Data Cleaning:** Standardizing text data to a consistent format.
**2. Text Transformation:** Preparing data for systems or applications that are case-sensitive.
**3. Data Analysis:** Ensuring uniformity in text data before analysis.
**4. Database Management:** Matching or comparing text values without being affected by text case.

---

## Step-by-Step Guide

**Step 1:** Open your Excel workbook and navigate to the worksheet where you want to use the `LOWER` function.

**Step 2:** Click on the cell where you want the lowercase text to appear.

**Step 3:** Enter the `LOWER` function. The syntax for the function is:

---

## =LOWER(text)

---

- `text` is the text string or cell reference you want to convert to lowercase.

**Step 4:** After entering the desired text or cell reference, press `Enter`. Excel will display the text in lowercase in the selected cell.

---

### Example

### Downloadable example:
https://tinyurl.com/102-excel-functions

Imagine you're managing a customer database, and you've received names of new customers. However, the names are in a mix of uppercase and proper case. You want to standardize all names to lowercase for consistency.

Data:

A1: Customer Name
A2: JOHN DOE
A3: Jane Smith
A4: ALICE Johnson

| | A |
|---|---|
| 1 | Customer Name |
| 2 | JOHN DOE |
| 3 | Jane Smith |
| 4 | ALICE Johnson |

**Step 1:** Click on cell B1 and type "Lowercase Name" as the header.

| | A | B |
|---|---|---|
| 1 | Customer Name | Lowercase Name |
| 2 | JOHN DOE | |
| 3 | Jane Smith | |
| 4 | ALICE Johnson | |

**Step 2:** In cell B2, enter the `LOWER` function to convert the name in A2 to lowercase:

=LOWER(A2)

| | A | B |
|---|---|---|
| 1 | Customer Name | Lowercase Name |
| 2 | JOHN DOE | =LOWER(A2) |
| 3 | Jane Smith | |
| 4 | ALICE Johnson | |

**Step 3:** Press `Enter`. Excel will display the result "john doe" in B2.

| | A | B |
|---|---|---|
| 1 | Customer Name | Lowercase Name |
| 2 | JOHN DOE | john doe |
| 3 | Jane Smith | |
| 4 | ALICE Johnson | |

**Step 4:** Drag the fill handle (a small square at the bottom-right corner of the cell) down from B2 to B4 to apply the `LOWER` function to the rest of the names. The results will be:

B2: john doe
B3: jane smith
B4: alice johnson

| | A | B |
|---|---|---|
| 1 | Customer Name | Lowercase Name |
| 2 | JOHN DOE | john doe |
| 3 | Jane Smith | jane smith |
| 4 | ALICE Johnson | alice johnson |

**Note:** If you need to convert text to uppercase, you can use the `UPPER` function. For converting text to proper case (where the first letter of each word is capitalized), you can use the `PROPER` function.

# Function #23 - COUNTBLANK

The `COUNTBLANK` function in Excel counts the number of empty cells in a specified range. This function is particularly beneficial in various scenarios:

**1. Data Cleaning:** Identifying missing or incomplete data in datasets.

**2. Survey Analysis:** Counting unanswered questions or responses in a survey.

**3. Inventory Management:** Identifying items or products without certain details.

**4. Attendance Tracking:** Counting days when no entry was made, indicating potential absences.

---

## Step-by-Step Guide

**Step 1:** Open your Excel workbook and navigate to the worksheet where you want to use the `COUNTBLANK` function.

**Step 2:** Click on the cell where you want the count of blank cells to appear.

**Step 3:** Enter the `COUNTBLANK` function. The syntax for the function is:

---

## =COUNTBLANK(range)

---

- `range` is the range of cells you want to count the blank cells in.

**Step 4:** After entering the desired range, press `Enter`. Excel will display the count of blank cells in the selected range.

---

### Example

### Downloadable example:
https://tinyurl.com/102-excel-functions

Imagine you're a teacher who has recorded the test scores of students. Some students missed the test, so their scores are blank. You want to find out how many students missed the test.

Data:

A1: Student Name   B1: Test Score
A2: John          B2: 85
A3: Jane          B3:
A4: Alice         B4: 90
A5: Bob           B5:
A6: Charlie       B6: 78

| | A | B | |
|---|---|---|---|
| 1 | Student Name | Test Score | |
| 2 | John | 85 | |
| 3 | Jane | | |
| 4 | Alice | 90 | |
| 5 | Bob | | |
| 6 | Charlie | 78 | |

**Step 1:** Click on cell C1 and type "Number of Students Absent".

| | A | B | C |
|---|---|---|---|
| 1 | Student Name | Test Score | Number of Students Absent |
| 2 | John | 85 | |
| 3 | Jane | | |
| 4 | Alice | 90 | |
| 5 | Bob | | |
| 6 | Charlie | 78 | |

**Step 2:** In cell C2, enter the `COUNTBLANK` function to count the blank cells in the "Test Score" column:

=COUNTBLANK(B2:B6)

| | A | B | C |
|---|---|---|---|
| 1 | Student Name | Test Score | Number of Students Absent |
| 2 | John | 85 | =COUNTBLANK(B2:B6) |
| 3 | Jane | | |
| 4 | Alice | 90 | |
| 5 | Bob | | |
| 6 | Charlie | 78 | |

**Step 3:** Press `Enter`. Excel will display the result `2` in C2, indicating that two students missed the test.

| | A | B | C |
|---|---|---|---|
| 1 | Student Name | Test Score | Number of Students Absent |
| 2 | John | 85 | 2 |
| 3 | Jane | | |
| 4 | Alice | 90 | |
| 5 | Bob | | |
| 6 | Charlie | 78 | |

**Note:** It's important to differentiate between cells that are truly blank and those that might contain invisible characters, such as spaces. The `COUNTBLANK` function will only count cells that are entirely empty.

# Function #24 - SEARCH

The `SEARCH` function in Excel is used to find the position of a specific substring within a text string. It returns the starting position of the first occurrence of the substring. This function is case-insensitive and allows for wildcard characters. It's especially beneficial in various scenarios:

**1. Data Analysis:** Identifying the presence of specific keywords or patterns in text data.

**2. Text Transformation:** Extracting or replacing parts of a text string based on specific criteria.

**3. Data Validation:** Checking for specific formats or patterns in data entries.

**4. Database Management:** Filtering or categorizing records based on text content.

---

### Step-by-Step Guide

**Step 1:** Open your Excel workbook and navigate to the worksheet where you want to use the `SEARCH` function.

**Step 2:** Click on the cell where you want the position of the substring to appear.

**Step 3:** Enter the `SEARCH` function. The syntax for the function is:

---

**=SEARCH(find_text, within_text, [start_num])**

---

- `find_text` is the text you want to find.
- `within_text` is the text in which you want to search for `find_text`.
- `start_num` (optional) is the position in `within_text` where you want to start the search. If omitted, it defaults to 1.

> ➢ **Depending on your country, the ' , ' must be replaced by ' ; '**

**Step 4:** After entering the required text values and starting position (if needed), press `Enter`. Excel will display the starting position of the substring in the selected cell.

---

**Example**

**Downloadable example:**
https://tinyurl.com/102-excel-functions

Imagine you're analyzing customer feedback and want to find out if the word "excellent" appears in a given comment and at what position.

Data:

A1: Feedback
A2: The product quality is excellent and I love it.

| | A |
|---|---|
| 1 | Feedback |
| 2 | The product quality is excellent and I love it. |

**Step 1:** Click on cell B1 and type "Position of 'excellent'".

| | A | B |
|---|---|---|
| 1 | Feedback | Position of excellent |
| 2 | The product quality is excellent and I love it. | |

**Step 2:** In cell B2, enter the `SEARCH` function to find the position of the word "excellent" in the feedback:

=SEARCH("excellent", A2)

| | A | B |
|---|---|---|
| 1 | Feedback | Position of excellent |
| 2 | The product quality is excellent and I love it. | =SEARCH("excellent"; A2) |

**Step 3:** Press `Enter`. Excel will display the result `24` in B2, indicating that the word "excellent" starts at the 24th character of the feedback.

| | A | B |
|---|---|---|
| 1 | Feedback | Position of excellent |
| 2 | The product quality is excellent and I love it. | 24 |

---

**Advanced Tips:**

**1. Case-Insensitive:** Remember that `SEARCH` is case-insensitive. If you need a case-sensitive search, consider using the `FIND` function.

**2. Using Wildcards:** `SEARCH` allows for wildcards. The question mark (?) matches any single character, and the asterisk (*) matches any sequence of characters. For example, `=SEARCH("ex*nt", A2)` would still find "excellent".

---

102

# Function #25 - HLOOKUP

The `HLOOKUP` function in Excel stands for "Horizontal Lookup." It's used to search for a value in the top row of a table or array and then return a value in the same column from a specified row. This function is especially beneficial in various scenarios:

**1. Data Retrieval:** Extracting associated data from a horizontal table based on a specific lookup value.
**2. Grade Systems:** Finding grades or remarks from horizontal grading tables.
**3. Pricing Tables:** Retrieving prices or details from product tables arranged horizontally.
**4. Financial Analysis:** Extracting financial metrics from horizontal financial tables.

While `VLOOKUP` is more commonly used for vertical lookups, `HLOOKUP` is essential when dealing with data arranged in rows rather than columns.

## Step-by-Step Guide

**Step 1:** Open your Excel workbook and navigate to the worksheet where you want to use the `HLOOKUP` function.

**Step 2:** Click on the cell where you want the retrieved data to appear.

**Step 3:** Enter the `HLOOKUP` function. The syntax for the function is:

---

**=HLOOKUP(lookup_value, table_array, row_index_num, [range_lookup])**

---

- `lookup_value` is the value you want to search for.
- `table_array` is the table or array where you want to find the data.
- `row_index_num` is the row number in the table or array from which you want to retrieve the data.
- `range_lookup` (optional) is a logical value that specifies whether you want `HLOOKUP` to find an exact match or an approximate match. If TRUE or omitted, an approximate match is returned. If FALSE, an exact match is returned.

> ➤ **Depending on your country, the ' , ' must be replaced by ' ; '**

**Step 4:** After entering the required values and ranges, press `Enter`. Excel will display the corresponding value in the selected cell.

## Example

### Downloadable example:
https://tinyurl.com/102-excel-functions

Imagine you're a store manager with a horizontal price table for different products. You want to find the price of a product in a specific month.

Data:

A1: Product    B1: January    C1: February    D1: March
A2: Shoes    B2: $50    C2: $55    D2: $52
A3: Bags    B3: $40    C3: $42    D3: $43
A4: Shirts    B4: $20    C4: $22    D4: $21

| | A | B | C | D |
|---|---|---|---|---|
| 1 | Product | January | February | March |
| 2 | Shoes | $50 | $55 | $52 |
| 3 | Bags | $40 | $42 | $43 |
| 4 | Shirts | $20 | $22 | $21 |

**Step 1:** In cell F1, type "Product" and in F2, enter "Shoes".

| | A | B | C | D | E | F |
|---|---|---|---|---|---|---|
| 1 | Product | January | February | March | | Product |
| 2 | Shoes | $50 | $55 | $52 | | Shoes |
| 3 | Bags | $40 | $42 | $43 | | |
| 4 | Shirts | $20 | $22 | $21 | | |

**Step 2:** In cell G1, type "Month" and in G2, enter "February".

**Step 3:** In cell H1, type "Price".

| | A | B | C | D | E | F | G |
|---|---|---|---|---|---|---|---|
| 1 | Product | January | February | March | | Product | Month |
| 2 | Shoes | $50 | $55 | $52 | | Shoes | February |
| 3 | Bags | $40 | $42 | $43 | | | |
| 4 | Shirts | $20 | $22 | $21 | | | |

**Step 4:** In cell H2, enter the `HLOOKUP` function to find the price of "Shoes" in "February":

=HLOOKUP(G2, B1:D4, MATCH(F2, A1:A4, 0), FALSE)

| | A | B | C | D | E | F | G | H | I | J | K | L |
|---|---|---|---|---|---|---|---|---|---|---|---|---|
| 1 | Product | January | February | March | | Product | Month | | | | | |
| 2 | Shoes | $50 | $55 | $52 | | Shoes | February | =HLOOKUP(G2; B1:D4; MATCH(F2; A1:A4; 0); FALSE) | | | | |
| 3 | Bags | $40 | $42 | $43 | | | | | | | | |
| 4 | Shirts | $20 | $22 | $21 | | | | | | | | |

**Step 5:** Press `Enter`. Excel will display the result `$55` in H2, indicating the price of "Shoes" in February.

| | A | B | C | D | E | F | G | H |
|---|---|---|---|---|---|---|---|---|
| 1 | Product | January | February | March | | Product | Month | |
| 2 | Shoes | $50 | $55 | $52 | | Shoes | February | $55 |
| 3 | Bags | $40 | $42 | $43 | | | | |
| 4 | Shirts | $20 | $22 | $21 | | | | |

> **Note:** Ensure that the `lookup_value` is in the top row of the `table_array`. If your data is vertically arranged, consider using `VLOOKUP` instead.

# Function #26 - COLUMN

The `COLUMN` function in Excel returns the column number of a specified cell reference. If no cell reference is provided, it returns the column number of the cell in which the function resides. This function is especially beneficial in various scenarios:

**1. Dynamic Formulas:** Adjusting formulas based on the position of a cell.
**2. Data Analysis:** Creating formulas that react to the structure of your data.
**3. Array Formulas:** Working with arrays where column positions matter.
**4. Cell Referencing:** Identifying the column number of a particular cell, which can be useful in various lookup and reference functions.

---

### Step-by-Step Guide

**Step 1:** Open your Excel workbook and navigate to the worksheet where you want to use the `COLUMN` function.

**Step 2:** Click on the cell where you want the column number to appear.

**Step 3:** Enter the `COLUMN` function. The syntax for the function is:

| =COLUMN([reference]) |
|:---:|

- `reference` (optional) is the cell reference for which you want to find the column number. If omitted, the function will return the column number of the cell in which it resides.

**Step 4:** After entering the desired cell reference (or leaving it blank), press `Enter`. Excel will display the column number in the selected cell.

---

**Example**

**Downloadable example:**
https://tinyurl.com/102-excel-functions

Imagine you're working on a spreadsheet with various data columns, and you want to identify the column numbers for specific cells to help with a data analysis task.

Data Layout:

A1: Name   B1: Age   C1: Occupation

| | A | B | C |
|---|---|---|---|
| 1 | Name | Age | Occupation |

**Step 1:** Click on cell E1 and type "Column Number for".

| | A | B | C | D | E |
|---|---|---|---|---|---|
| 1 | Name | Age | Occupation | | Column Number for |
| 2 | | | | | |
| 3 | | | | | |

**Step 2:** In cell E2, type "Occupation".

| | A | B | C | D | E |
|---|---|---|---|---|---|
| 1 | Name | Age | Occupation | | Column Number for |
| 2 | | | | | Occupation |
| 3 | | | | | |

**Step 3:** In cell F1, type "Result".

| | A | B | C | D | E | F |
|---|---|---|---|---|---|---|
| 1 | Name | Age | Occupation | | Column Number for | Result |
| 2 | | | | | Occupation | |
| 3 | | | | | | |

**Step 4:** In cell F2, enter the `COLUMN` function to find the column number for "Occupation":

=COLUMN(C1)

| | A | B | C | D | E | F |
|---|---|---|---|---|---|---|
| 1 | Name | Age | Occupation | | Column Number for | |
| 2 | | | | | Occupation | =COLUMN(C1) |

**Step 5:** Press `Enter`. Excel will display the result `3` in F2, indicating that "Occupation" is in the third column.

| | A | B | C | D | E | F |
|---|---|---|---|---|---|---|
| 1 | Name | Age | Occupation | | Column Number for | Result |
| 2 | | | | | Occupation | 3 |
| 3 | | | | | | |

**Advanced Usage:**

**1. Relative Positioning:** If you use the `COLUMN` function without any argument, it will return the column number of the cell it's in. For example, if you place `=COLUMN()` in cell D5, it will return `4` because D is the fourth column.

**2. Dynamic Column Referencing:** Combined with other functions, `COLUMN` can be used to create dynamic formulas. For instance, `INDEX(A1:C3, 2,COLUMN()-1)` would return the value from the second row of the column one to the left of the cell containing the formula.

# Function #27 - ROUNDUP

The `ROUNDUP` function in Excel rounds a number up to a specified number of digits. This function is especially beneficial in various scenarios:

**1. Financial Calculations:** Ensuring values are always rounded up, such as when calculating interest or taxes.

**2. Inventory Management:** Rounding up quantities to ensure adequate stock.

**3. Data Analysis:** Standardizing numerical data for consistency in reports.

**4. Mathematical Computations:** Achieving precision in mathematical models and simulations.

---

**Step-by-Step Guide**

**Step 1:** Open your Excel workbook and navigate to the worksheet where you want to use the `ROUNDUP` function.

**Step 2:** Click on the cell where you want the rounded number to appear.

**Step 3:** Enter the `ROUNDUP` function. The syntax for the function is:

## =ROUNDUP(number, num_digits)

- `number` is the value you want to round up.
- `num_digits` specifies the number of digits to which you want to round the number. If `num_digits` is greater than 0 (zero), then the number is rounded to the specified number of decimal places. If `num_digits` is 0, the number is rounded to the nearest integer. If `num_digits` is less than 0, the number is rounded to the left of the decimal point.

➢ **Depending on your country, the ' , ' must be replaced by ' ; '**

**Step 4:** After entering the desired number and number of digits, press `Enter`. Excel will display the rounded number in the selected cell.

---

## Example

**Downloadable example:**
https://tinyurl.com/102-excel-functions

Imagine you're a manufacturer calculating the amount of material needed for a product. Each product requires 2.34 meters of material. You always want to ensure you have enough material, so you always round up to the nearest meter.

Data:

A1: Product    B1: Material Needed (meters)
A2: Widget A    B2: 2.34

| | A | B |
|---|---|---|
| 1 | Product | Material Needed (meters) |
| 2 | Widget A | 2,34 |

**Step 1:** Click on cell C1 and type "Rounded Material Needed".

| | A | B | C |
|---|---|---|---|
| 1 | Product | Material Needed (meters) | Rounded Material Needed |
| 2 | Widget A | 2,34 | |

**Step 2:** In cell C2, enter the `ROUNDUP` function to round up the material needed for "Widget A":

=ROUNDUP(B2, 0)

| | A | B | C |
|---|---|---|---|
| 1 | Product | Material Needed (meters) | |
| 2 | Widget A | 2,34 | =ROUNDUP(B2; 0) |

**Step 3:** Press `Enter`. Excel will display the result `3` in C2, indicating that you'll need 3 meters of material for "Widget A" when rounding up.

| | A | B | C |
|---|---|---|---|
| 1 | Product | Material Needed (meters) | Rounded Material Needed |
| 2 | Widget A | 2,34 | 3 |

**Advanced Tips:**

**1. Rounding to Tens or Hundreds:** If you want to round up to the nearest ten, you'd use a `num_digits` value of -1. For rounding up to the nearest hundred, you'd use -2, and so on.

**2. Difference with ROUND:** While `ROUND` rounds numbers based on standard rounding rules (i.e., values ending in .5 and above are rounded up, and below .5 are rounded down), `ROUNDUP` always rounds numbers up.

# Function #28 - WEEKNUM

The `WEEKNUM` function in Excel returns the week number of a specific date in a year. This function is especially beneficial in various scenarios:

**1. Project Management:** Tracking project progress by weeks.
**2. Sales Analysis:** Analyzing weekly sales data.
**3. Attendance Tracking:** Monitoring weekly attendance or logins.
**4. Event Planning:** Organizing events based on week numbers.
**5. Reporting:** Generating weekly reports.

---

**Step-by-Step Guide**

**Step 1:** Open your Excel workbook and navigate to the worksheet where you want to use the `WEEKNUM` function.

**Step 2:** Click on the cell where you want the week number to appear.

**Step 3:** Enter the `WEEKNUM` function. The syntax for the function is:

---

### =WEEKNUM(serial_number, [return_type])

---

- `serial_number` is the date for which you want to find the week number.
- `return_type` (optional) is a number that determines which day of the week should be considered the start of the week. If omitted, it defaults to 1 (Sunday).

> ➤ **Depending on your country, the ' , ' must be replaced by ' ; '**

**Step 4:** After entering the desired date and return type (if needed), press `Enter`. Excel will display the week number in the selected cell.

---

## Example

**Downloadable example:**
https://tinyurl.com/102-excel-functions

Imagine you're a teacher planning lessons for the year. You want to know which week of the year a particular date falls on to align with your curriculum.

Data:

A1: Date        B1: 15-Jan-2023

| | A | B |
|---|---|---|
| 1 | Date | 15-janv-23 |
| 2 | | |

**Step 1:** Click on cell C1 and type "Week Number".

| | A | B | C |
|---|---|---|---|
| 1 | Date | 15-janv-23 | Week Number |
| 2 | | | |

**Step 2:** In cell C2, enter the `WEEKNUM` function to find the week number for the date in B1:

=WEEKNUM(B1, 2)
Here, the `return_type` is set to 2, which means the week starts on Monday.

| | A | B | C |
|---|---|---|---|
| 1 | Date | 15-janv-23 | |
| 2 | | | =WEEKNUM(B1; 2) |
| 3 | | | |

**Step 3:** Press `Enter`. Excel will display the result `3` in C2, indicating that January 15, 2023, falls in the third week of the year when considering Monday as the start of the week.

| | A | B | C |
|---|---|---|---|
| 1 | Date | 15-janv-23 | Week Number |
| 2 | | | 3 |

---

### Advanced Tips:

**1. Different Start Days:** The `return_type` can be any number from 1 to 21, each representing different start days and week numbering systems. For instance, a `return_type` of 1 starts the week on Sunday, while 2 starts the week on Monday.

**2. ISO Week Number:** If you want to get the ISO week number (where the week starts on a Monday and the first week of the year contains January 4), you can use `return_type` 21.

---

# Function #29 - INT

The `INT` function in Excel rounds a number down to the nearest integer. This function is especially beneficial in various scenarios:

**1. Financial Calculations:** Truncating decimal values to get whole numbers.
**2. Inventory Management:** Rounding down quantities to ensure no fractional units.
**3. Data Analysis:** Standardizing numerical data for consistency in reports.
**4. Mathematical Computations:** Achieving precision in mathematical models by removing fractional parts.

---

## Step-by-Step Guide

**Step 1:** Open your Excel workbook and navigate to the worksheet where you want to use the `INT` function.

**Step 2:** Click on the cell where you want the rounded number to appear.

**Step 3:** Enter the `INT` function. The syntax for the function is:

| =INT(number) |
|---|

- `number` is the value you want to round down to the nearest integer.

**Step 4:** After entering the desired number, press `Enter`. Excel will display the rounded number in the selected cell.

---

**Example**

**Downloadable example:**
https://tinyurl.com/102-excel-functions

Imagine you're a factory manager calculating the number of products that can be made from a given amount of raw material. Each product requires 2.5 units of material. You want to know how many whole products can be made without considering the fractional product.

Data:

A1: Raw Material Units   B1: 17,8

| | A | B |
|---|---|---|
| 1 | Raw Material Units | 17,8 |

**Step 1:** Click on cell C1 and type "Whole Products".

| | A | B | C |
|---|---|---|---|
| 1 | Raw Material Units | 17,8 | Whole Products |

**Step 2:** In cell C2, enter a formula to calculate the number of products that can be made:

=B1/2,5

This will give you the result `7,12`.

| | A | B | C |
|---|---|---|---|
| 1 | Raw Material Units | 17,8 | Whole Products |
| 2 | | | 7,12 |

Step 3: To get the number of whole products, in cell D1 type "Rounded Down Products". In cell D2, enter the `INT` function:

=INT(C2)

| | A | B | C | D |
|---|---|---|---|---|
| 1 | Raw Material Units | 17,8 | Whole Products | |
| 2 | | | 7,12 | =INT(C2) |

**Step 4:** Press `Enter`. Excel will display the result `7` in D2, indicating that you can make 7 whole products from the given raw material.

| | A | B | C | D |
|---|---|---|---|---|
| 1 | Raw Material Units | 17,8 | Whole Products | |
| 2 | | | 7,12 | 7 |

**Note:** The `INT` function always rounds down, regardless of the decimal value. If you need to round to the nearest whole number based on standard rounding rules, consider using the `ROUND` function.

# Function #30 - MONTH

The `MONTH` function in Excel returns the month as a number (1 for January to 12 for December) from a given date. This function is especially beneficial in various scenarios:

**1. Financial Analysis:** Grouping data by month for monthly reports or forecasts.
**2. Sales Tracking:** Analyzing monthly sales trends.
**3. Event Planning:** Extracting the month from event dates for planning purposes.
**4. Data Cleaning:** Standardizing date data by isolating the month component.
**5. Scheduling & Calendars**: Building dynamic calendars and schedules.

---

## Step-by-Step Guide

**Step 1:** Open your Excel workbook and navigate to the worksheet where you want to use the `MONTH` function.

**Step 2:** Click on the cell where you want the month number to appear.

**Step 3:** Enter the `MONTH` function. The syntax for the function is:

---

### =MONTH(serial_number)

---

- `serial_number` is the date from which you want to extract the month.

**Step 4:** After entering the desired date, press `Enter`. Excel will display the month number in the selected cell.

---

### Example

**Downloadable example:**
https://tinyurl.com/102-excel-functions

Imagine you're an event manager with a list of event dates. You want to categorize these events by the month in which they occur.

Data:

A1: Event Date     B1: 15-Mar-2023

| | A | B |
|---|---|---|
| 1 | Event Date | 15-mars-23 |
| 2 | | |
| 3 | | |

**Step 1:** Click on cell C1 and type "Event Month".

| | A | B | C |
|---|---|---|---|
| 1 | Event Date | 15-mars-23 | Event Month |
| 2 | | | |

**Step 2:** In cell C2, enter the `MONTH` function to extract the month from the event date:

=MONTH(B1)

| | A | B | C |
|---|---|---|---|
| 1 | Event Date | 15-mars-23 | |
| 2 | | | =MONTH(B1) |
| 3 | | | |

**Step 3:** Press `Enter`. Excel will display the result `3` in C2, indicating that the event is in March, the third month of the year.

| | A | B | C |
|---|---|---|---|
| 1 | Event Date | 15-mars-23 | Event Month |
| 2 | | | 3 |
| 3 | | | |

**Advanced Tips:**

**1. Formatting:** While the `MONTH` function returns a number, you can use custom formatting or other functions like `TEXT` to display the month name instead of the number.

**2. Year and Day:** To extract the year and day from a date, you can use the `YEAR` and `DAY` functions, respectively.

**3. Dynamic Date Input:** The `MONTH` function can be combined with other date functions like `TODAY()` to work with the current date. For example, `=MONTH(TODAY())` would return the current month's number.

# Function #31 - SMALL

The `SMALL` function in Excel returns the k-th smallest value from a data set. This function is especially beneficial in various scenarios:

1. **Data Analysis:** Identifying the top or bottom values in a dataset.
2. **Ranking & Scoring:** Determining the nth smallest score or rank.
3. **Inventory Management:** Identifying the lowest stock levels.
4. **Financial Analysis:** Extracting the lowest values from financial data.
5. **Reporting:** Highlighting specific percentile data points.

---

## Step-by-Step Guide

**Step 1:** Open your Excel workbook and navigate to the worksheet where you want to use the `SMALL` function.

**Step 2:** Click on the cell where you want the nth smallest value to appear.

**Step 3:** Enter the `SMALL` function. The syntax for the function is:

| =SMALL(array, k) |
|---|

- `array` is the range of data from which you want to retrieve the k-th smallest value.
- `k` specifies the position from the smallest value you want to retrieve.

> ➢ **Depending on your country, the ' , ' must be replaced by ' ; '**

Step 4: After entering the desired range and k value, press `Enter`. Excel will display the k-th smallest value in the selected cell.

---

## Example

### Downloadable example:
https://tinyurl.com/102-excel-functions

Imagine you're a teacher who has just graded a test. You want to know the second and third lowest scores from the test results.

Data:

A1: Student Scores

A2: 85

A3: 78

A4: 90

A5: 82

A6: 88

A7: 79

| | A |
|---|---|
| 1 | Student Scores |
| 2 | 85 |
| 3 | 78 |
| 4 | 90 |
| 5 | 82 |
| 6 | 88 |
| 7 | 79 |

**Step 1:** Click on cell B1 and type "2nd Lowest Score".

| | A | B |
|---|---|---|
| 1 | Student Scores | 2nd Lowest Score |
| 2 | 85 | |
| 3 | 78 | |
| 4 | 90 | |
| 5 | 82 | |
| 6 | 88 | |
| 7 | 79 | |

**Step 2:** In cell B2, enter the `SMALL` function to find the second lowest score:

=SMALL(A2:A7, 2)

| | A | B |
|---|---|---|
| 1 | Student Scores | |
| 2 | 85 | =SMALL(A2:A7; 2) |
| 3 | 78 | |
| 4 | 90 | |
| 5 | 82 | |
| 6 | 88 | |
| 7 | 79 | |

**Step 3:** Press `Enter`. Excel will display the result `79` in B2, indicating that the second lowest score is 79.

| | A | B |
|---|---|---|
| 1 | Student Scores | 2nd Lowest Score |
| 2 | 85 | 79 |
| 3 | 78 | |
| 4 | 90 | |
| 5 | 82 | |
| 6 | 88 | |
| 7 | 79 | |

**Step 4:** Similarly, to find the third lowest score, click on cell C1 and type "3rd Lowest Score". In cell C2, enter:

=SMALL(A2:A7, 3)

After pressing `Enter`, Excel will display the result `82`, indicating the third lowest score.

| | A | B |
|---|---|---|
| 1 | Student Scores | 2nd Lowest Score |
| 2 | 85 | 82 |
| 3 | 78 | |
| 4 | 90 | |
| 5 | 82 | |
| 6 | 88 | |
| 7 | 79 | |

**Advanced Tips:**

**1. Largest Values:** If you're interested in the largest values, consider using the `LARGE` function, which works similarly but retrieves the k-th largest values.

**2. Dynamic Positioning:** The k value can be a reference to another cell, allowing for dynamic extraction of positions. For instance, if you have a cell where users can input a number, you can reference that cell as the k value to get the nth smallest score based on user input.

# Function #32 - CONCATENATE

The `CONCATENATE` function in Excel is used to combine multiple text strings into one. This function is especially beneficial in various scenarios:

**1. Data Presentation:** Combining first and last names, addresses, or other data for display.
**2. File Path Creation:** Constructing file paths by combining folder and file names.
**3. Data Cleaning:** Merging data from multiple columns into a standardized format.
**4. Reporting:** Creating custom messages or labels based on data.

---

**Step-by-Step Guide**

**Step 1:** Open your Excel workbook and navigate to the worksheet where you want to use the `CONCATENATE` function.

**Step 2:** Click on the cell where you want the combined text to appear.

**Step 3:** Enter the `CONCATENATE` function. The syntax for the function is:

| =CONCATENATE(text1, [text2], ...) |

- `text1, text2, ...` are the text strings or ranges of cells you want to combine.

> **Depending on your country, the ' , ' must be replaced by ' ; '**

**Step 4:** After entering the desired text strings or cell references, press `Enter`. Excel will display the combined text in the selected cell.

---

## Example

**Downloadable example:**
https://tinyurl.com/102-excel-functions

Imagine you're an HR manager with a list of employees' first and last names in separate columns. You want to create a single column with their full names.

Data:

A1: First Name    B1: Last Name
A2: John        B2: Doe
A3: Jane        B3: Smith

A4: Robert     B4: Johnson

| | A | B |
|---|---|---|
| 1 | First Name | Last Name |
| 2 | John | Doe |
| 3 | Jane | Smith |
| 4 | Robert | Johnson |

**Step 1:** Click on cell C1 and type "Full Name".

| | A | B | C |
|---|---|---|---|
| 1 | First Name | Last Name | Full Name |
| 2 | John | Doe | |
| 3 | Jane | Smith | |
| 4 | Robert | Johnson | |

**Step 2:** In cell C2, enter the `CONCATENATE` function to combine the first and last names:

=CONCATENATE(A2, " ", B2)

| | A | B | C |
|---|---|---|---|
| 1 | First Name | Last Name | Full Name |
| 2 | John | Doe | =CONCATENATE(A2;" ";B2) |
| 3 | Jane | Smith | |
| 4 | Robert | Johnson | |

The space between the quotation marks (" ") ensures there's a space between the first and last names.

**Step 3:** Press `Enter`. Excel will display the result `John Doe` in C2.

| | A | B | C |
|---|---|---|---|
| 1 | First Name | Last Name | Full Name |
| 2 | John | Doe | John Doe |
| 3 | Jane | Smith | |
| 4 | Robert | Johnson | |

**Step 4:** Drag the formula down in column C to apply it to the other rows. Cells C3 and C4 will display `Jane Smith` and `Robert Johnson`, respectively.

| | A | B | C |
|---|---|---|---|
| 1 | First Name | Last Name | Full Name |
| 2 | John | Doe | John Doe |
| 3 | Jane | Smith | Jane Smith |
| 4 | Robert | Johnson | Robert Johnson |

**Advanced Tips:**

**1. Ranges:** `CONCATENATE` can also combine ranges. For example, `=CONCATENATE(A2:A4)` would produce `JohnJaneRobert`.

**2. Special Characters:** You can include special characters or symbols in the combination. For instance, to separate names with a comma, you'd use `=CONCATENATE(A2, ", ", B2)`.

**3. Alternative Function:** Excel also offers the `TEXTJOIN` function, which provides more flexibility by allowing you to set a delimiter and ignore empty cells.

# Function #33 - EXACT

The `EXACT` function in Excel is used to compare two text strings and determine if they are exactly the same. This function is case-sensitive, making it especially beneficial in various scenarios:

**1. Data Validation:** Ensuring consistency in data entries.
**2. Password Verification:** Checking if entered passwords match the original.
**3. Data Cleaning:** Identifying discrepancies in data due to case differences.
**4. Duplicate Checking:** Comparing entries to find exact matches.

---

## Step-by-Step Guide

**Step 1:** Open your Excel workbook and navigate to the worksheet where you want to use the `EXACT` function.

**Step 2:** Click on the cell where you want the comparison result to appear.

**Step 3:** Enter the `EXACT` function. The syntax for the function is:

---

## =EXACT(text1, text2)

---

- `text1` and `text2` are the two text strings you want to compare.

> ➤ **Depending on your country, the ' , ' must be replaced by ' ; '**

**Step 4:** After entering the desired text strings or cell references, press `Enter`. Excel will display `TRUE` if the strings are exactly the same and `FALSE` if they are not.

---

### Example

**Downloadable example:**
https://tinyurl.com/102-excel-functions

Imagine you're managing a registration system. Users are required to enter their email twice for verification. You want to check if both entries match exactly.

Data:

A1: Email Entry 1    B1: Email Entry 2
A2: JohnDoe@email.com B2: johndoe@email.com

A3:          JaneSmith@email.com        B3:
JaneSmith@email.com

| | A | B |
|---|---|---|
| 1 | Email Entry | Email Entry |
| 2 | JohnDoe@email.com | johndoe@email.com |
| 3 | JaneSmith@email.com | JaneSmith@email.com |

**Step 1:** Click on cell C1 and type "Exact Match?".

| | A | B | C |
|---|---|---|---|
| 1 | Email Entry | Email Entry | Exact Match |
| 2 | JohnDoe@email.com | johndoe@email.com | |
| 3 | JaneSmith@email.com | JaneSmith@email.com | |

**Step 2:** In cell C2, enter the `EXACT` function to compare the two email entries:

=EXACT(A2, B2)

| | A | B | C |
|---|---|---|---|
| 1 | Email Entry | Email Entry | Exact Match |
| 2 | JohnDoe@email.com | johndoe@email.com | =EXACT(A2; B2) |
| 3 | JaneSmith@email.com | JaneSmith@email.com | |

**Step 3:** Press `Enter`. Excel will display the result `FALSE` in C2 because the function is case-sensitive and the two email entries are not exactly the same in terms of case.

141

| | A | B | C |
|---|---|---|---|
| 1 | Email Entry | Email Entry | Exact Match |
| 2 | JohnDoe@email.com | johndoe@email.com | FALSE |
| 3 | JaneSmith@email.com | JaneSmith@email.com | |

**Step 4:** Drag the formula down in column C to apply it to the other rows. Cell C3 will display `TRUE` because the two email entries in row 3 match exactly.

| | A | B | C |
|---|---|---|---|
| 1 | Email Entry | Email Entry | Exact Match |
| 2 | JohnDoe@email.com | johndoe@email.com | FALSE |
| 3 | JaneSmith@email.com | JaneSmith@email.com | TRUE |

## Advanced Tips:

**1. Case-Insensitive Comparison:** If you want a case-insensitive comparison, consider using a formula like `=UPPER(A2)=UPPER(B2)` or `=LOWER(A2)=LOWER(B2)`.

**2. Combining with Conditional Formatting:** You can use the `EXACT` function with conditional formatting to highlight cells that don't have exact matches, making it easier to spot discrepancies.

# Function #34 - ISBLANK

The `ISBLANK` function in Excel is used to determine if a cell is empty or not. This function is especially beneficial in various scenarios:

**1. Data Validation:** Identifying missing data in a dataset.

**2. Conditional Formatting:** Highlighting empty cells for attention or action.

**3. Data Cleaning:** Filtering out or replacing blank cells with default values.

**4. Formulas & Calculations:** Preventing errors in calculations by checking for blank inputs.

**5. Reporting:** Creating dynamic reports that adjust based on the presence or absence of data.

---

**Step-by-Step Guide**

**Step 1:** Open your Excel workbook and navigate to the worksheet where you want to use the `ISBLANK` function.

**Step 2:** Click on the cell where you want the result (TRUE or FALSE) to appear.

**Step 3:** Enter the `ISBLANK` function. The syntax for the function is:

---
**=ISBLANK(reference)**
---

- `reference` is the cell you want to check for emptiness.

**Step 4:** After entering the desired cell reference, press `Enter`. Excel will display `TRUE` if the cell is empty and `FALSE` if it contains any value (including spaces, numbers, text, or other data).

---

**Example**

**Downloadable example:**
https://tinyurl.com/102-excel-functions

Imagine you're a school administrator with a list of student names and their corresponding grades. You want to identify if any grades are missing.

Data:

A1: Student Name    B1: Grade
A2: John Doe        B2: 85
A3: Jane Smith      B3:
A4: Robert Johnson  B4: 90

| | A | B |
|---|---|---|
| 1 | Student Name | Grade |
| 2 | John Doe | 85 |
| 3 | Jane Smith | |
| 4 | Robert Johnson | 90 |

**Step 1:** Click on cell C1 and type "Grade Missing?".

| | A | B | C |
|---|---|---|---|
| 1 | Student Name | Grade | Grade Missing? |
| 2 | John Doe | 85 | |
| 3 | Jane Smith | | |
| 4 | Robert Johnson | 90 | |

**Step 2:** In cell C2, enter the `ISBLANK` function to check if the grade for John Doe is missing:

=ISBLANK(B2)

| | A | B | C |
|---|---|---|---|
| 1 | Student Name | Grade | Grade Missing? |
| 2 | John Doe | 85 | =ISBLANK(B2) |
| 3 | Jane Smith | | |
| 4 | Robert Johnson | 90 | |

**Step 3:** Press `Enter`. Excel will display the result `FALSE` in C2 because John Doe has a grade entered.

| | A | B | C |
|---|---|---|---|
| 1 | Student Name | Grade | Grade Missing? |
| 2 | John Doe | 85 | FALSE |
| 3 | Jane Smith | | |
| 4 | Robert Johnson | 90 | |

**Step 4:** Drag the formula down in column C to apply it to the other rows. Cell C3 will display `TRUE` because Jane Smith's grade is missing, while C4 will display `FALSE`.

| | A | B | C |
|---|---|---|---|
| 1 | Student Name | Grade | Grade Missing? |
| 2 | John Doe | 85 | FALSE |
| 3 | Jane Smith | | TRUE |
| 4 | Robert Johnson | 90 | FALSE |

**Advanced Tips:**

**1. Combining with Conditional Formatting:** Use the `ISBLANK` function with conditional formatting to automatically highlight cells in column B that are missing grades.

**2. Using with IF Statements:** You can combine `ISBLANK` with the `IF` function to display custom messages or values. For example, `=IF(ISBLANK(B2), "Enter Grade", "Grade Entered")` would display "Enter Grade" for blank cells and "Grade Entered" for cells with grades.

**3. Difference with "":** While `ISBLANK` checks for truly empty cells, sometimes cells might appear empty but contain invisible characters like spaces. In such cases, you might use a formula like `=B2=""` to check for cells that appear empty.

# Function #35 - ISTEXT

The `ISTEXT` function in Excel is used to determine if a cell contains text. This function is especially beneficial in various scenarios:

**1. Data Validation:** Ensuring that certain cells have text entries and not numbers or other data types.
**2. Data Cleaning:** Identifying and handling cells that contain unexpected text in a dataset expected to have numbers.
**3. Conditional Formatting:** Highlighting cells that contain text for clarity or action.
**4. Data Analysis:** Categorizing data based on whether it's textual or numeric.
**5. Formulas & Calculations:** Preventing errors in calculations by checking for text inputs.

---

**Step-by-Step Guide**

**Step 1:** Open your Excel workbook and navigate to the worksheet where you want to use the `ISTEXT` function.

**Step 2:** Click on the cell where you want the result (TRUE or FALSE) to appear.

**Step 3:** Enter the `ISTEXT` function. The syntax for the function is:

| =ISTEXT(reference) |
| --- |

- `reference` is the cell you want to check for text content.

**Step 4:** After entering the desired cell reference, press `Enter`. Excel will display `TRUE` if the cell contains text and `FALSE` if it does not.

---

## Example

**Downloadable example:**
https://tinyurl.com/102-excel-functions

Imagine you're an accountant with a list of transaction amounts. However, some cells might contain text notes instead of numbers. You want to identify these cells.

Data:

A1: Transaction Amount
A2: 150,25
A3: Refunded
A4: 200,50

| | A |
|---|---|
| 1 | Transaction Amount |
| 2 | 150,25 |
| 3 | Refunded |
| 4 | 200,5 |

**Step 1:** Click on cell B1 and type "Contains Text?".

| | A | B |
|---|---|---|
| 1 | Transaction Amount | Contains Text? |
| 2 | 150,25 | |
| 3 | Refunded | |
| 4 | 200,5 | |

**Step 2:** In cell B2, enter the `ISTEXT` function to check if the transaction amount is text:

=ISTEXT(A2)

| | A | B |
|---|---|---|
| 1 | Transaction Amount | Contains Text? |
| 2 | 150,25 | =ISTEXT(A2) |
| 3 | Refunded | |
| 4 | 200,5 | |

**Step 3:** Press `Enter`. Excel will display the result `FALSE` in B2 because the cell contains a number.

|   | A | B |
|---|---|---|
| 1 | Transaction Amount | Contains Text? |
| 2 | 150,25 | FALSE |
| 3 | Refunded | |
| 4 | 200,5 | |

**Step 4:** Drag the formula down in column B to apply it to the other rows. Cell B3 will display `TRUE` because it contains the text "Refunded", while B4 will display `FALSE`.

|   | A | B |
|---|---|---|
| 1 | Transaction Amount | Contains Text? |
| 2 | 150,25 | FALSE |
| 3 | Refunded | TRUE |
| 4 | 200,5 | FALSE |

## Advanced Tips:

**1. Combining with Conditional Formatting:** Use the `ISTEXT` function with conditional formatting to automatically highlight cells in column A that contain text.

**2. Using with IF Statements:** You can combine `ISTEXT` with the `IF` function to display custom messages or values. For example, `=IF(ISTEXT(A2), "Check Entry", "Valid")` would display "Check Entry" for text cells and "Valid" for numeric cells.

**3. Other IS Functions:** Excel provides a range of similar functions like `ISNUMBER`, `ISERROR`, and `ISBLANK` to check for other data types or conditions.

# Function #36 - MID

The `MID` function in Excel is used to extract a specific substring from a text string, starting at any position you specify. This function is especially beneficial in various scenarios:

**1. Data Cleaning:** Extracting specific portions of data from a larger text string.

**2. Text Analysis:** Analyzing and categorizing data based on specific text patterns.

**3. Data Transformation:** Creating new data columns based on specific parts of existing text data.

**4. Reporting:** Extracting key information from text-based reports.

**5. Parsing Data:** Breaking down complex strings into more manageable or understandable parts.

---

## Step-by-Step Guide

**Step 1:** Open your Excel workbook and navigate to the worksheet where you want to use the `MID` function.

**Step 2:** Click on the cell where you want the extracted text to appear.

**Step 3:** Enter the `MID` function. The syntax for the function is:

| =MID(text, start_num, num_chars) |
|---|

- `text` is the original text string from which you want to extract.
- `start_num` is the position in the text string where you want to start extraction.
- `num_chars` is the number of characters you want to extract.

> ➢ **Depending on your country, the ' , ' must be replaced by ' ; '**

**Step 4:** After entering the desired parameters, press `Enter`. Excel will display the extracted substring in the selected cell.

---

**Example**

**Downloadable example:**
https://tinyurl.com/102-excel-functions

Imagine you're managing a database of product codes. Each code has a format "XXX-YYYY-ZZZZ", where XXX is the product category, YYYY is the product

ID, and ZZZZ is the batch number. You want to extract the product ID from these codes.

Data:

A1: Product Code
A2: ABC-1234-5678
A3: DEF-5678-1234
A4: GHI-9012-3456

| | A |
|---|---|
| 1 | Product Code |
| 2 | ABC-1234-5678 |
| 3 | DEF-5678-1234 |
| 4 | GHI-9012-3456 |

**Step 1:** Click on cell B1 and type "Product ID".

| | A | B |
|---|---|---|
| 1 | Product Code | Product ID |
| 2 | ABC-1234-5678 | |
| 3 | DEF-5678-1234 | |
| 4 | GHI-9012-3456 | |

**Step 2:** In cell B2, enter the `MID` function to extract the product ID:

=MID(A2, 5, 4)

| ⊿ | A | B |
|---|---|---|
| 1 | Product Code | Product ID |
| 2 | ABC-1234-5678 | =MID(A2; 5; 4) |
| 3 | DEF-5678-1234 | |
| 4 | GHI-9012-3456 | |

This formula starts extracting from the 5th character and takes 4 characters, which corresponds to the product ID.

**Step 3:** Press `Enter`. Excel will display the result `1234` in B2.

| ⊿ | A | B |
|---|---|---|
| 1 | Product Code | Product ID |
| 2 | ABC-1234-5678 | 1234 |
| 3 | DEF-5678-1234 | |
| 4 | GHI-9012-3456 | |

**Step 4:** Drag the formula down in column B to apply it to the other rows. Cells B3 and B4 will display `5678` and `9012`, respectively.

| ⊿ | A | B |
|---|---|---|
| 1 | Product Code | Product ID |
| 2 | ABC-1234-5678 | 1234 |
| 3 | DEF-5678-1234 | 5678 |
| 4 | GHI-9012-3456 | 9012 |

**Advanced Tips:**

**1. Dynamic Extraction:** The `MID` function can be combined with other functions like `SEARCH` or `FIND` to determine the start position dynamically based on specific characters or patterns.

**2. Error Handling:** If the `start_num` is greater than the length of the text, or if `num_chars` specifies more characters than are available, `MID` will return a shorter string or an empty string without causing an error.

**3. Related Functions:** `LEFT` and `RIGHT` are two other functions in Excel that allow you to extract substrings from the beginning or end of a text string, respectively.

# Function #37 - REPLACE

The `REPLACE` function in Excel is used to replace part of a text string with another text string. This function is especially beneficial in various scenarios:

**1. Data Cleaning:** Modifying incorrect or outdated parts of data entries.

**2. Text Transformation:** Updating specific portions of text based on new information or standards.

**3. Data Formatting:** Adjusting text data to fit a particular format or template.

**4. Data Anonymization:** Replacing sensitive information with placeholders or generic data.

**5. Pattern Alteration:** Changing recurring patterns or codes within larger text datasets.

---

### Step-by-Step Guide

**Step 1:** Open your Excel workbook and navigate to the worksheet where you want to use the `REPLACE` function.

**Step 2:** Click on the cell where you want the modified text to appear.

**Step 3:** Enter the `REPLACE` function. The syntax for the function is:

| =REPLACE(old_text, start_num, num_chars, new_text) |
|---|

- `old_text` is the original text string that you want to modify.
- `start_num` is the position in the text string where you want to start the replacement.
- `num_chars` is the number of characters in the old text that you want to replace.
- `new_text` is the text that will replace the characters in the old text.

> ➢ **Depending on your country, the ' , ' must be replaced by ' ; '**

**Step 4:** After entering the desired parameters, press `Enter`. Excel will display the modified text in the selected cell.

---

**Example**

**Downloadable example:**
https://tinyurl.com/102-excel-functions

Imagine you're managing a database of product codes. Each code has a format "XXX-YYYY", where XXX is the country code and YYYY is the product ID. Due to a change in country coding standards, you need to replace "USA" with "US" in all product codes.

Data:

A1: Product Code
A2: USA-1234
A3: USA-5678
A4: CAN-9012

| | A |
|---|---|
| 1 | Product Code |
| 2 | USA-1234 |
| 3 | USA-5678 |
| 4 | CAN-9012 |

**Step 1:** Click on cell B1 and type "Updated Code".

| | A | B |
|---|---|---|
| 1 | Product Code | Updated Code |
| 2 | USA-1234 | |
| 3 | USA-5678 | |
| 4 | CAN-9012 | |

**Step 2:** In cell B2, enter the `REPLACE` function to update the country code:

=REPLACE(A2, 1, 3, "US")

| | A | B | C |
|---|---|---|---|
| 1 | Product Code | Updated Code | |
| 2 | USA-1234 | =REPLACE(A2; 1; 3; "US") | |
| 3 | USA-5678 | | |
| 4 | CAN-9012 | | |

This formula starts the replacement at the 1st character, replaces the next 3 characters (USA), and substitutes them with "US".

**Step 3:** Press `Enter`. Excel will display the result `US-1234` in B2.

| | A | B |
|---|---|---|
| 1 | Product Code | Updated Code |
| 2 | USA-1234 | US-1234 |
| 3 | USA-5678 | |
| 4 | CAN-9012 | |

**Step 4:** Drag the formula down in column B to apply it to the other rows. Cell B3 will display `US-5678`, while B4 remains unchanged as `CAN-9012` since it didn't have the "USA" prefix.

| | A | B |
|---|---|---|
| 1 | Product Code | Updated Code |
| 2 | USA-1234 | US-1234 |
| 3 | USA-5678 | US-5678 |
| 4 | CAN-9012 | US-9012 |

**Advanced Tips:**

**1. Dynamic Replacement:** The `REPLACE` function can be combined with functions like `SEARCH` or `FIND` to determine the start position dynamically based on specific characters or patterns.

**2. Related Functions:** `SUBSTITUTE` is another function in Excel that allows you to replace all occurrences of a specified substring with another substring.

**3. Error Handling:** If the `start_num` is greater than the length of the text, or if `num_chars` specifies more characters than are available, `REPLACE` will still insert the `new_text` at the specified position.

# Function #38 - SUMIFS

The `SUMIFS` function in Excel is used to sum values in a range based on one or more criteria. It's an extension of the simpler `SUMIF` function, which sums based on a single condition. The benefits of `SUMIFS` include:

**1. Data Analysis:** Easily aggregate data based on specific conditions.
**2. Financial Reporting:** Sum financial data based on categories, dates, or other criteria.
**3. Inventory Management:** Calculate total quantities or values based on product types, dates, or other filters.
**4. Performance Tracking:** Sum scores or results based on multiple conditions.
**5. Data Validation:** Ensure data integrity by checking aggregated values against expected totals.

---

### Step-by-Step Guide

**Step 1:** Open your Excel workbook and navigate to the worksheet containing the data you want to sum.

**Step 2:** Click on the cell where you want the summed result to appear.

**Step 3:** Enter the `SUMIFS` function. The syntax for the function is:

> =SUMIFS(sum_range, criteria_range1, criteria1, [criteria_range2, criteria2], ...)

- `sum_range` is the range of cells you want to sum.
- `criteria_range1` is the range of cells you want to evaluate against `criteria1`.
- `criteria1` is the condition you want to apply to `criteria_range1`.
- Additional criteria ranges and criteria can be added as needed.

> ➢ **Depending on your country, the ' , ' must be replaced by ' ; '**

**Step 4:** After entering the desired ranges and criteria, press `Enter`. Excel will display the summed value based on the specified conditions.

---

**Example**

**Downloadable example:**
https://tinyurl.com/102-excel-functions

Imagine you're managing sales data for a store. You want to calculate the total sales for a specific product category in a specific month.

Data:

A1: Date      B1: Category    C1: Sales
A2: Jan    B2:A     C2: 100
A3: Jan    B3: B    C3: 150
A4: Feb    B4: A    C4: 110
A5: Jan    B5: A    C5: 120

| | A | B | C |
|---|---|---|---|
| 1 | Date | Category | Sales |
| 2 | Jan | A | 100 |
| 3 | Jan | B | 150 |
| 4 | Feb | A | 110 |
| 5 | Jan | A | 120 |

**Step 1:** Click on cell D1 and type "Total Sales for Product A in January".

| | A | B | C | D | E |
|---|---|---|---|---|---|
| 1 | Date | Category | Sales | | Total Sales for Product A in January |
| 2 | Jan | A | 100 | | |
| 3 | Jan | B | 150 | | |
| 4 | Feb | A | 110 | | |
| 5 | Jan | A | 120 | | |

**Step 2:** In cell D2, enter the `SUMIFS` function to calculate the total sales for the Product A in January:

=SUMIFS(C2:C5, A2:A5, "Jan",B2:B5,"A")

165

| | A | B | C | D | E | F |
|---|---|---|---|---|---|---|
| 1 | Date | Category | Sales | Total Sales for Product A in January | | |
| 2 | Jan | A | 100 | =SUMIFS(C2:C5; A2:A5; "Jan";B2:B5;"A") | | |
| 3 | Jan | B | 150 | | | |
| 4 | Feb | A | 110 | | | |
| 5 | Jan | A | 120 | | | |

**Step 3:** Press `Enter`. Excel will display the result `220` in D2, which is the total sales for Product A in January.

| | A | B | C | D | E | |
|---|---|---|---|---|---|---|
| 1 | Date | Category | Sales | Total Sales for Product A in January | | |
| 2 | Jan | A | 100 | 220 | | |
| 3 | Jan | B | 150 | | | |
| 4 | Feb | A | 110 | | | |
| 5 | Jan | A | 120 | | | |

---

**Advanced Tips:**

**1. Using Cell References:** Instead of hardcoding criteria like "Electronics", you can use cell references. This makes your formula dynamic and easily adjustable.

**2. Wildcards:** In your criteria, you can use wildcards like `*` (for a sequence of characters) and `?` (for a single character) to make more flexible conditions.

**3. Other Functions:** `SUMIFS` can be combined with other functions for more advanced calculations. For example, you might use `DATE` functions to generate date criteria dynamically.

**4. Criteria Operators:** You can use operators like `>`, `<`, `>=`, `<=`, and `<>` to create conditions based on numerical or date values.

---

# Function #39 - DAYS360

The DAYS360 function in Excel is a financial function that calculates the number of days between two dates based on a 360-day year. This 360-day year assumption is commonly used in some financial markets, notably in bond markets. The function provides a standardized way of calculating day counts for financial transactions. The benefits of `DAYS360` include:

**1. Standardization:** Adheres to the financial industry's 360-day year convention.

**2. Simplicity:** Easily calculate the number of days between two dates without manual counting.

**3. Accuracy:** Provides consistent results for financial calculations.

**4. Versatility:** Useful for various financial scenarios, including interest calculations and bond pricing.

---

**Step-by-Step Guide**

**Step 1:** Understanding the Syntax:

| DAYS360(start_date, end_date, [method]) |
| --- |

- start_date: The start date.
- end_date: The end date.

- method: An optional logical value: TRUE for the European method or FALSE for the U.S. method. If omitted, the U.S. method is used.

➢ **Depending on your country, the ' , ' must be replaced by ' ; '**

**Step 2:** Click on the cell where you want the result. Start typing =DAYS360( and input the necessary arguments..

**Step 3:** Choosing the Method:

- U.S. method (default): If both dates are the last day of February, the day of month is changed to 30. Otherwise, if the start date is the last day of a month, it's changed to 30. If the end date is the last day of a month and the start date is earlier than the 30th, the end date's day is changed to 1 of the next month, otherwise, it's changed to 30.

- European method: All days in all months are treated as if they occur on the 30th.

**Step 4 :** The function will return the number of days between the two dates based on the 360-day year convention.

## Example

**Downloadable example:**
https://tinyurl.com/102-excel-functions

Imagine you want to calculate the number of days between January 1 and December 31 using the U.S. method.

=DAYS360(DATE(2022,1,1), DATE(2022,12,31))

| | A | B | C | D | E |
|---|---|---|---|---|---|
| 1 | =DAYS360(DATE( 2022;1;1 ); DATE( 2022;12;31 )) | | | | |
| 2 | | | | | |
| 3 | | | | | |

The result would display 360 days.

| | A | B |
|---|---|---|
| 1 | 360 | |
| 2 | | |
| 3 | | |

For the European method:

=DAYS360(DATE(2022,1,1),     DATE(2022,12,31), TRUE)

The result would still display 360 days in this case, but differences might appear in other scenarios due to the method's day-counting rules.

**Advanced Tips:**

**1. Consider the Context:** Always be aware of the context in which you're using the DAYS360 function. While it's standard in some financial sectors, it might not be appropriate for other scenarios where actual day counts are needed.

**2. Cross-check with Other Methods:** If you're unsure about the results from DAYS360, cross-check with the simple subtraction of end date minus start date. This will give you the actual day difference, which you can compare with the 360-day convention.

**3. Use with Other Functions:** Combine DAYS360 with other Excel functions for more complex calculations. For example, to calculate simple interest: =DAYS360(start_date, end_date) * rate/360 * principal.

# Function #40 - MIN

The `MIN` function in Excel is used to determine the smallest number in a given set of values. This function is especially beneficial in various scenarios:

**1. Data Analysis:** Quickly identify the lowest value in a dataset.

**2. Performance Tracking:** Determine the lowest score, time, or other performance metrics.

**3. Financial Analysis:** Identify the lowest sales, revenue, or other financial figures in a given period.

**4. Inventory Management:** Find the product with the least stock.

**5. Reporting:** Highlight or report on minimum values for presentations or summaries.

---

### Step-by-Step Guide

**Step 1:** Open your Excel workbook and navigate to the worksheet containing the data you want to analyze.

**Step 2:** Click on the cell where you want the minimum value to appear.

**Step 3:** Enter the `MIN` function. The syntax for the function is:

| =MIN(number1, [number2], ...) |
|---|

- `number1, number2, ...` are the numbers or ranges you want to find the minimum value from.

> ➤ **Depending on your country, the ' , ' must be replaced by ' ; '**

**Step 4:** After entering the desired numbers or ranges, press `Enter`. Excel will display the smallest number among the provided values.

---

**Example**

**Downloadable example:**
https://tinyurl.com/102-excel-functions

Imagine you're a teacher who has just graded a series of tests. You want to identify the lowest score in the class to understand the range of performance.

Data:

A1: Student Names    B1: Scores

A2: Alice    B2: 85

A3: Bob      B3: 78

A4: Charlie  B4: 92

A5: Dana     B5: 81

| | A | B |
|---|---|---|
| 1 | Student Name | Scores |
| 2 | Alice | 85 |
| 3 | Bob | 78 |
| 4 | Charlie | 92 |
| 5 | Dana | 81 |

**Step 1:** Click on cell B6 and type "Lowest Score".

| | A | B |
|---|---|---|
| 1 | Student Name | Scores |
| 2 | Alice | 85 |
| 3 | Bob | 78 |
| 4 | Charlie | 92 |
| 5 | Dana | 81 |
| 6 | | Lowest Score |

**Step 2:** In cell B7, enter the `MIN` function to determine the lowest score:

=MIN(B2:B5)

| | A | B | C |
|---|---|---|---|
| 1 | Student Name | Scores | |
| 2 | Alice | 85 | |
| 3 | Bob | 78 | |
| 4 | Charlie | 92 | |
| 5 | Dana | 81 | |
| 6 | | Lowest Score | =MIN(B2:B5) |

**Step 3:** Press `Enter`. Excel will display the result `78` in B7, which is the lowest score in the class.

| | A | B | C |
|---|---|---|---|
| 1 | Student Name | Scores | |
| 2 | Alice | 85 | |
| 3 | Bob | 78 | |
| 4 | Charlie | 92 | |
| 5 | Dana | 81 | |
| 6 | | Lowest Score | 78 |

---

**Advanced Tips:**

**1. Ignoring Non-Numeric Data:** The `MIN` function automatically ignores text, logical values, or empty cells in the range.

**2. Combining with Other Functions:** You can use the `MIN` function alongside other functions like `IF` to find minimum values based on certain conditions.

**3. Related Functions:**
   - `MAX`: Finds the highest value in a dataset.
   - `MINA`: Similar to `MIN`, but it also considers logical values and text (representing them as numbers).

**4. Array Formulas:** With array formulas, you can use `MIN` to find the smallest value based on multiple conditions without needing helper columns.

---

# Function #41 - IFS

The `IFS` function in Excel is used to evaluate multiple conditions and return a value corresponding to the first TRUE condition. It's essentially a streamlined way to use multiple `IF` statements without nesting them. The benefits of `IFS` include:

**1. Simplicity:** Reduces the complexity of formulas by avoiding nested `IF` statements.
**2. Readability:** Makes formulas easier to read and understand, especially when dealing with multiple conditions.
**3. Efficiency:** Evaluates conditions in order, stopping once it finds the first TRUE condition, which can improve calculation times in large datasets.
**4. Error Reduction:** Minimizes the chances of missing or misplacing parentheses, which is common in nested `IF` statements.

---

### Step-by-Step Guide

**Step 1:** Open your Excel workbook and navigate to the worksheet where you want to use the `IFS` function.

**Step 2:** Click on the cell where you want the result to appear.

**Step 3:** Enter the `IFS` function. The syntax for the function is:

=IFS(condition1, value1, [condition2, value2], ...)

- `condition1, condition2, ...` are the conditions you want to evaluate.
- `value1, value2, ...` are the corresponding values or actions to return if the respective condition is TRUE.

> **Depending on your country, the ' , ' must be replaced by ' ; '**

**Step 4:** After entering the desired conditions and values, press `Enter`. Excel will display the value corresponding to the first TRUE condition.

---

## Example

**Downloadable example:**
https://tinyurl.com/102-excel-functions

Imagine you're a teacher grading assignments. You want to assign letter grades based on the following criteria:
- 90 and above: A
- 80 to 89: B
- 70 to 79: C
- 60 to 69: D
- Below 60: F

Data:

A1: Student Names   B1: Scores   C1: Grade
A2: Alice           B2: 85       C2: ?
A3: Bob             B3: 92       C3: ?
A4: Charlie         B4: 75       C4: ?

| | A | B | C |
|---|---|---|---|
| 1 | Student Name | Scores | Grade |
| 2 | Alice | 85 | |
| 3 | Bob | 92 | |
| 4 | Charlie | 75 | |

**Step 1:** Click on cell C2.

**Step 2:** Enter the `IFS` function to determine the letter grade for Alice:

=IFS(B2>=90, "A", B2>=80, "B", B2>=70, "C", B2>=60, "D", B2<60, "F")

178

**Step 3:** Press `Enter`. Excel will display the result `B` in C2, which is the grade for Alice.

**Step 4:** Drag the formula down in column C to apply it to the other students. Cells C3 and C4 will display `A` and `C`, respectively.

---

**Advanced Tips:**

**1. Order Matters:** The `IFS` function evaluates conditions in the order they're provided. Once it finds a TRUE condition, it returns the corresponding value and stops evaluating.

**2. Handling No Match:** If none of the conditions are TRUE, the `IFS` function will return a `#N/A` error. You can handle this using the `IFERROR` function.

**3. Combining with Other Functions:** You can use other functions within the `IFS` function to create more complex conditions or return values.

---

# Function #42 - EDATE

The `EDATE` function in Excel is used to add or subtract a specified number of months to a given date, returning a new date as a result. This function is especially beneficial in various scenarios:

**1. Financial Planning:** Calculate maturity dates for investments or loans.

**2. Project Management:** Determine start or end dates based on project timelines.

**3. Event Planning:** Schedule recurring events, like monthly meetings or annual celebrations.

**4. Inventory Management:** Calculate expiration dates for products with a specific shelf life.

**5. Reporting:** Generate reports for specific fiscal quarters or periods.

---

## Step-by-Step Guide

**Step 1:** Open your Excel workbook and navigate to the worksheet where you want to use the `EDATE` function.

**Step 2:** Click on the cell where you want the calculated date to appear.

**Step 3:** Enter the `EDATE` function. The syntax for the function is:

| =EDATE(start_date, months) |
|---|

- `start_date` is the original date you want to modify.
- `months` is the number of months you want to add (positive value) or subtract (negative value) from the `start_date`.

> ➢ **Depending on your country, the ' , ' must be replaced by ' ; '**

**Step 4:** After entering the desired date and number of months, press `Enter`. Excel will display the new date based on the specified criteria.

---

**Example**

**Downloadable example:**
https://tinyurl.com/102-excel-functions

Imagine you're managing a subscription service where customers sign up for 6-month contracts. You want to determine the end date of the contract based on the start date.

Data:

A1: Customer Name    B1: Start Date    C1: Contract
End Date
A2: Alice          B2: 15/01/23    C2: ?
A3: Bob            B3: 02/10/23    C3: ?

| | A | B | C | D |
|---|---|---|---|---|
| 1 | Customer Name | Start Date | Contract End Date | |
| 2 | Alice | 15/01/2023 | | |
| 3 | Bob | 10/02/2023 | | |

**Step 1:** Click on cell C2.

**Step 2:** Enter the `EDATE` function to determine the contract end date for Alice:

=EDATE(B2, 6)

| | A | B | C | D |
|---|---|---|---|---|
| 1 | Customer Name | Start Date | Contract End Date | |
| 2 | Alice | 15/01/2023 | =EDATE(B2; 6) | |
| 3 | Bob | 10/02/2023 | | |

This formula adds 6 months to Alice's start date.

Step 3: Press `Enter`. Excel will display the result `15/07/23` in C2, which is the contract end date for Alice.

| | A | B | C | D |
|---|---|---|---|---|
| 1 | Customer Name | Start Date | Contract End Date | |
| 2 | Alice | 15/01/2023 | 15/07/2023 | |
| 3 | Bob | 10/02/2023 | | |
| 4 | | | | |

Step 4: Drag the formula down in column C to apply it to the other customers. Cell C3 will display `10/08/23`, which is the contract end date for Bob.

| | A | B | C | D |
|---|---|---|---|---|
| 1 | Customer Name | Start Date | Contract End Date | |
| 2 | Alice | 15/01/2023 | 15/07/2023 | |
| 3 | Bob | 10/02/2023 | 10/08/2023 | |

**Advanced Tips:**

**1. Handling Invalid Dates:** If the resulting date is an invalid date (e.g., April 31), `EDATE` will automatically adjust to the next valid date (e.g., May 1).

**2. Year Adjustments:** The `EDATE` function can cross year boundaries. For example, adding 12 months to a date in January 2023 will result in a date in January 2024.

**3. Combining with Other Functions:** You can use the `EDATE` function alongside other date functions, like `DAY`, `MONTH`, or `YEAR`, to create more complex date calculations.

183

# Function #43 - LEFT

The `LEFT` function in Excel is used to retrieve a specific number of characters from the start (or left side) of a text string. This function is especially beneficial in various scenarios:

**1. Data Cleaning:** Extract relevant portions of data from larger text strings.

**2. Text Analysis:** Break down text into smaller components for analysis.

**3. Data Formatting:** Prepare data for reports, presentations, or further processing.

**4. ID Parsing:** Extract specific parts of identification numbers or codes.

**5. File Naming:** Extract prefixes or identifiers from file names.

---

## Step-by-Step Guide

**Step 1:** Open your Excel workbook and navigate to the worksheet where you want to use the `LEFT` function.

**Step 2:** Click on the cell where you want the extracted text to appear.

**Step 3:** Enter the `LEFT` function. The syntax for the function is:

**=LEFT(text, [num_chars])**

- `text` is the original text string from which you want to extract characters.
- `num_chars` is the number of characters you want to extract from the left side of the `text`. If omitted, it defaults to 1.

> ➢ **Depending on your country, the ' , ' must be replaced by ' ; '**

Step 4: After entering the desired text and number of characters, press `Enter`. Excel will display the extracted text based on the specified criteria.

---

**Example**

**Downloadable example:**
https://tinyurl.com/102-excel-functions

Imagine you're managing a list of product codes where each code starts with a two-letter category identifier. You want to extract just the category identifier from each code.

Data:

A1: Product Code   B1: Category Identifier

A2: EL12345        B2: ?

A3: TO98765        B3: ?

A4: AP56432        B4: ?

| | A | B | C |
|---|---|---|---|
| 1 | Product Code | Category Identifier | |
| 2 | EL12345 | | |
| 3 | TO98765 | | |
| 4 | AP56432 | | |

**Step 1:** Click on cell B2.

**Step 2:** Enter the `LEFT` function to extract the category identifier for the first product code:

=LEFT(A2, 2)

| | A | B |
|---|---|---|
| 1 | Product Code | Category Identifier |
| 2 | EL12345 | =LEFT(A2; 2) |
| 3 | TO98765 | |
| 4 | AP56432 | |

This formula extracts the first 2 characters from the product code in cell A2.

**Step 3:** Press `Enter`. Excel will display the result `EL` in B2, which is the category identifier for the first product.

| | A | B |
|---|---|---|
| 1 | Product Code | Category Identifier |
| 2 | EL12345 | EL |
| 3 | TO98765 | |
| 4 | AP56432 | |

**Step 4:** Drag the formula down in column B to apply it to the other product codes. Cells B3 and B4 will display `TO` and `AP`, respectively.

| | A | B |
|---|---|---|
| 1 | Product Code | Category Identifier |
| 2 | EL12345 | EL |
| 3 | TO98765 | TO |
| 4 | AP56432 | AP |
| 5 | | |

---

**Advanced Tips:**

**1. Combining with Other Functions:** You can use the `LEFT` function alongside other text functions, like `LEN`, to create dynamic extractions based on the length of the text.

**2. Error Handling:** If `num_chars` exceeds the length of the text, the `LEFT` function will simply return the entire text without causing an error.

**3. Right-Side Extraction:** For extracting characters from the end (or right side) of a text string, you can use the `RIGHT` function in Excel.

---

# Function #44 - ROW

The `ROW` function in Excel is used to retrieve the row number of a given cell reference. If no reference is provided, it returns the row number of the cell containing the formula. The benefits of the `ROW` function include:

**1. Dynamic Referencing:** Create formulas that adjust based on their position in the spreadsheet.
**2. Data Analysis:** Use in conjunction with other functions for advanced data manipulation and analysis.
**3. Array Formulas:** Essential for some array formulas where you need to generate a series of numbers.
**4. Cell Identification:** Quickly identify the row number of specific cells, especially in large datasets.

---

## Step-by-Step Guide

**Step 1:** Open your Excel workbook and navigate to the worksheet where you want to use the `ROW` function.

**Step 2:** Click on the cell where you want the row number to appear.

**Step 3:** Enter the `ROW` function. The syntax for the function is:

=ROW([reference])

- `reference` is the cell or range of cells for which you want the row number. If omitted, the function will return the row number of the cell containing the formula.

**Step 4:** After entering the desired reference (or leaving it blank), press `Enter`. Excel will display the row number based on the specified criteria.

---

## Example

**Downloadable example:**
https://tinyurl.com/102-excel-functions

Scenario: Imagine you're working with a dataset of products, and you want to add a column that indicates the row number for each product for easier reference.

Data:

A1: Product Name   B1: Row Number
A2: Laptop         B2: ?

A3: Mouse      B3: ?

A4: Keyboard      B4: ?

| | A | B |
|---|---|---|
| 1 | Product Name | Row Number |
| 2 | Laptop | |
| 3 | Mouse | |
| 4 | Keyboard | |

**Step 1:** Click on cell B2.

**Step 2:** Enter the `ROW` function without any reference to get the row number of the current cell:

=ROW()

| | A | B |
|---|---|---|
| 1 | Product Name | Row Number |
| 2 | Laptop | =ROW() |
| 3 | Mouse | |
| 4 | Keyboard | |
| 5 | | |

**Step 3:** Press `Enter`. Excel will display the result `2` in B2, which is the row number for the first product.

| | A | B |
|---|---|---|
| 1 | Product Name | Row Number |
| 2 | Laptop | 2 |
| 3 | Mouse | |
| 4 | Keyboard | |
| 5 | | |

**Step 4:** Drag the formula down in column B to apply it to the other products. Cells B3 and B4 will display `3` and `4`, respectively.

| | A | B |
|---|---|---|
| 1 | Product Name | Row Number |
| 2 | Laptop | 2 |
| 3 | Mouse | 3 |
| 4 | Keyboard | 4 |

---

**Advanced Tips:**

**1. Relative vs. Absolute:** The `ROW` function can be used with relative references (like A2) or absolute references (like $A$2). The latter can be useful when you don't want the reference to change as you copy the formula to other cells.

**2. Generating Series:** In combination with functions like `INDIRECT`, you can use the `ROW` function to generate a series of numbers.

**3. Array Formulas:** For advanced users, the `ROW` function can be a key component in array formulas, especially when working with dynamic ranges.

**4. Column Numbers:** If you're interested in column numbers instead of rows, you can use the `COLUMN` function in a similar manner.

# Function #45 - CHOOSE

The `CHOOSE` function in Excel is used to select one of up to 254 values based on an index number. Think of it as a way to create custom lookup tables directly within a formula. The benefits of the `CHOOSE` function include:

1. **Flexibility:** Easily return specific values or references based on an index without setting up a full lookup table.
2. **Simplicity:** Streamline formulas by embedding multiple options directly within the function.
3. **Dynamic Outputs:** Combine with other functions to produce dynamic results based on changing conditions.
4. **Data Transformation:** Convert numeric codes or indices into meaningful labels or values.

---

### Step-by-Step Guide

**Step 1:** Open your Excel workbook and navigate to the worksheet where you want to use the `CHOOSE` function.

**Step 2:** Click on the cell where you want the chosen value to appear.

**Step 3:** Enter the `CHOOSE` function. The syntax for the function is:

---

**=CHOOSE(index_num, value1, [value2], ...)**

---

- `index_num` is the position of the value you want to retrieve.
- `value1, value2, ...` are the list of values or references from which you want to choose.

> ➢ **Depending on your country, the ' , ' must be replaced by ' ; '**

**Step 4:** After entering the desired index and values, press `Enter`. Excel will display the value corresponding to the specified index.

---

## Example

**Downloadable example:**
https://tinyurl.com/102-excel-functions

Scenario: Imagine you're managing a coffee shop and have a code for each type of coffee. You want to convert these codes into the actual coffee names.

Data:

A1: Coffee Code   B1: Coffee Name
A2: 1            B2: ?
A3: 3            B3: ?
A4: 2            B4: ?

The codes represent:
1. Espresso
2. Cappuccino
3. Latte

| | A | B |
|---|---|---|
| 1 | Coffee Code | Coffee Name |
| 2 | 1 | |
| 3 | 3 | |
| 4 | 2 | |

**Step 1:** Click on cell B2.

**Step 2:** Enter the `CHOOSE` function to convert the coffee code into its name:

=CHOOSE(A2, "Espresso", "Cappuccino", "Latte")

| | A | B | C | D | E |
|---|---|---|---|---|---|
| 1 | Coffee Code | Coffee Name | | | |
| 2 | | 1 =CHOOSE(A2; "Espresso";"Cappuccino"; "Latte") | | | |
| 3 | | 3 | | | |
| 4 | | 2 | | | |

**Step 3:** Press `Enter`. Excel will display the result `Espresso` in B2, which corresponds to the code `1`.

**Step 4:** Drag the formula down in column B to apply it to the other coffee codes. Cells B3 and B4 will display `Latte` and `Cappuccino`, respectively.

| | A | B |
|---|---|---|
| 1 | Coffee Code | Coffee Name |
| 2 | 1 | Espresso |
| 3 | 3 | Latte |
| 4 | 2 | Cappuccino |

### Advanced Tips:

**1. Error Handling:** If the `index_num` is less than 1 or greater than the number of values listed, the `CHOOSE` function will return a `#VALUE!` error. Ensure your index is within the valid range.

**2. Dynamic Indexing:** The `index_num` can be a formula or reference to another cell, allowing for dynamic outputs based on changing conditions.

**3. Combining Functions:** You can use other functions as the values within `CHOOSE`, making it a powerful tool for complex calculations based on an index.

**4. Alternative Functions:** For more extensive lookup tasks, consider using functions like `VLOOKUP` or `INDEX` combined with `MATCH`.

# Function #46 - WORKDAY

The `WORKDAY` function in Excel is used to compute a date that is a specified number of working days ahead or behind a given start date. By default, it considers Saturday and Sunday as weekends. The primary benefits of the `WORKDAY` function include:

**1. Project Management:** Calculate project end dates based on working days, excluding weekends and holidays.

**2. Task Scheduling:** Determine when tasks or deliverables are due, considering only business days.

**3. Financial Planning:** Compute maturity dates for financial instruments that consider business days.

**4. Event Planning:** Schedule business events or meetings avoiding weekends and holidays.

5. Efficiency: Automate date calculations without manually counting days on a calendar.

---

## Step-by-Step Guide

**Step 1:** Open your Excel workbook and navigate to the worksheet where you want to use the `WORKDAY` function.

**Step 2:** Click on the cell where you want the calculated date to appear.

**Step 3:** Enter the `WORKDAY` function. The syntax for the function is:

---

**=WORKDAY(start_date, days, [holidays])**

---

- `start_date` is the starting date.
- `days` is the number of working days before (negative value) or after (positive value) the start date.
- `holidays` (optional) is a range of dates that should be excluded from the working calendar, in addition to the default weekends.

> ➤ **Depending on your country, the ' , ' must be replaced by ' ; '**

**Step 4:** After entering the required parameters, press `Enter`. Excel will display the calculated date based on the specified criteria.

---

## Example

### Downloadable example:
https://tinyurl.com/102-excel-functions

Imagine you're a project manager, and a project starts on 1st March 2023. The project is expected to last 15 working days. However, there are two public holidays within this period: 5th March and 12th March. You want to determine the project's end date.

Data:

A1: Start Date    B1: 01/03/2023
A2: Duration      B2: 15
A3: Holidays      B3: 05/03/2023
              B4: 12/03/2023
A5: End Date     B5: ?

| | A | B |
|---|---|---|
| 1 | Start Date | 01/03/2023 |
| 2 | Duration | 15 |
| 3 | Holidays | 05/03/2023 |
| 4 | | 12/03/2023 |
| 5 | End Date | |

**Step 1:** Click on cell B5.

**Step 2:** Enter the `WORKDAY` function to calculate the end date:

=WORKDAY(B1, B2, B3:B4)

| | A | B | C |
|---|---|---|---|
| 1 | Start Date | 01/03/2023 | |
| 2 | Duration | 15 | |
| 3 | Holidays | 05/03/2023 | |
| 4 | | 12/03/2023 | |
| 5 | End Date | =WORKDAY(B1; B2; B3:B4) | |

Step 3: Press `Enter`. Excel will display the result `22/03/2023` in B5, which is the project's end date, considering the working days and excluding weekends and the specified holidays.

| | A | B | |
|---|---|---|---|
| 1 | Start Date | 01/03/2023 | |
| 2 | Duration | 15 | |
| 3 | Holidays | 05/03/2023 | |
| 4 | | 12/03/2023 | |
| 5 | End Date | 22/03/2023 | |

**Advanced Tips:**

**1. Custom Weekends:** If your weekends are not the default Saturday and Sunday, consider using the `WORKDAY.INTL` function, which allows you to specify which days of the week should be considered weekends.

**2. Combining with Other Functions:** You can use the `WORKDAY` function alongside other date functions, like `EDATE` or `DATE`, to create more complex date calculations.

**3. Dynamic Scheduling:** Use cell references as arguments to make your `WORKDAY` calculations dynamic. For instance, changing the value in B2 (Duration) will automatically update the end date in B5.

# Function #47 - COUNTIF

The `COUNTIF` function in Excel is used to count the number of cells within a range that meet a single condition. This function is especially beneficial in various scenarios:

**1. Data Analysis:** Quickly determine the frequency of specific values in a dataset.

**2. Inventory Management:** Count items that meet certain criteria, such as items below a minimum stock level.

**3. Survey Analysis:** Tally responses that match a particular answer.

**4. Attendance Tracking:** Count the number of days an employee was absent or present.

**5. Quality Control:** Count items that pass or fail a test.

---

## Step-by-Step Guide

**Step 1:** Open your Excel workbook and navigate to the worksheet where you want to use the `COUNTIF` function.

**Step 2:** Click on the cell where you want the count to appear.

**Step 3:** Enter the `COUNTIF` function. The syntax for the function is:

---

| =COUNTIF(range, criteria) |
| --- |

---

- `range` is the group of cells you want to count.
- `criteria` is the condition you want to apply.

> ➤ **Depending on your country, the ' , ' must be replaced by ' ; '**

**Step 4:** After entering the desired range and criteria, press `Enter`. Excel will display the count of cells that meet the specified condition.

---

## Example

**Downloadable example:**
https://tinyurl.com/102-excel-functions

Imagine you're a teacher, and you have a list of student grades. You want to determine how many students scored above 90.

Data:

A1: Student Name   B1: Grade
A2: Alice          B2: 92
A3: Bob            B3: 85
A4: Charlie        B4: 93
A5: David          B5: 88
A6: Eve            B6: 91

| | A | B |
|---|---|---|
| 1 | Student Name | Grade |
| 2 | Alice | 92 |
| 3 | Bob | 85 |
| 4 | Charlie | 93 |
| 5 | David | 88 |
| 6 | Eve | 91 |
| 7 | | |

**Step 1:** Click on an empty cell, say C1.

**Step 2:** Enter the `COUNTIF` function to count the number of students who scored above 90:

=COUNTIF(B2:B6, ">90")

| | A | B | C | D |
|---|---|---|---|---|
| 1 | Student Name | Grade | =COUNTIF(B2:B6; ">90") | |
| 2 | Alice | 92 | | |
| 3 | Bob | 85 | | |
| 4 | Charlie | 93 | | |
| 5 | David | 88 | | |
| 6 | Eve | 91 | | |

**Step 3:** Press `Enter`. Excel will display the result `3` in C1, indicating that three students scored above 90.

| | A | B | C |
|---|---|---|---|
| 1 | Student Name | Grade | 3 |
| 2 | Alice | 92 | |
| 3 | Bob | 85 | |
| 4 | Charlie | 93 | |
| 5 | David | 88 | |
| 6 | Eve | 91 | |

## Advanced Tips:

**1. Using Wildcards:** The `COUNTIF` function supports wildcards. For instance, if you want to count cells containing text that starts with "A", you can use the criteria `"A*"`.

**2. Non-Text Criteria:** If your criteria is text that includes mathematical symbols (like `">90"`), enclose it in double quotes. But if it's a reference to another cell, you can combine them like `">"&C1`.

**3. Multiple Conditions:** If you need to count based on multiple conditions, consider using the `COUNTIFS` function.

**4. Case Sensitivity:** By default, `COUNTIF` is not case-sensitive. If you need a case-sensitive count, you'll need a more complex array formula or use other functions in combination.

# Function #48 - TEXTJOIN

The `TEXTJOIN` function in Excel is used to join multiple text strings into one text string. It's an enhancement over the older `CONCATENATE` function, offering more flexibility. The primary benefits of the `TEXTJOIN` function include:

**1. Delimiters:** Easily specify a delimiter, such as a comma or space, to separate the combined text.
**2. Ignore Empty Cells:** Has the option to ignore empty cells, which `CONCATENATE` can't do.
**3. Dynamic Ranges:** Can handle ranges of cells, making it more versatile than `CONCATENATE`.
**4. Data Cleaning:** Useful for merging data from different columns into a standardized format.

---

**Step-by-Step Guide**

**Step 1:** Open your Excel workbook and navigate to the worksheet where you want to use the `TEXTJOIN` function.

**Step 2:** Click on the cell where you want the combined text to appear.

**Step 3:** Enter the `TEXTJOIN` function. The syntax for the function is:

---
**=TEXTJOIN(delimiter, ignore_empty, text1, [text2], ...)**

---

- `delimiter` is the character(s) to separate the combined text.
- `ignore_empty` is a TRUE/FALSE value. If TRUE, the function will skip any empty cells.
- `text1, text2, ...` are the text items or ranges you want to combine.

➢ **Depending on your country, the ' , ' must be replaced by ' ; '**

**Step 4:** After entering the desired parameters, press `Enter`. Excel will display the combined text based on the specified criteria.

---

## Example

**Downloadable example:**
https://tinyurl.com/102-excel-functions

Imagine you're organizing a party and have a list of guests with their first and last names in separate columns. You want to create a single column with their full names, separated by a space.

Data:

A1: First Name  B1: Last Name  C1: Full Name
A2: John        B2: Doe        C2: ?
A3: Jane        B3: Smith      C3: ?
A4: Alice       B4: Johnson    C4: ?

| | A | B | C |
|---|---|---|---|
| 1 | First Name | Last Name | Full Name |
| 2 | John | Doe | |
| 3 | Jane | Smith | |
| 4 | Alice | Johnson | |

**Step 1:** Click on cell C2.

**Step 2:** Enter the `TEXTJOIN` function to combine the first and last names:

=TEXTJOIN(" ", TRUE, A2, B2)

**Step 3:** Press `Enter`. Excel will display the result `John Doe` in C2.

**Step 4:** Drag the formula down in column C to apply it to the other names. Cells C3 and C4 will display `Jane Smith` and `Alice Johnson`, respectively.

**Advanced Tips:**

**1. Using Delimiters:** You can use any character or set of characters as a delimiter. For example, to separate values with a comma and a space, use `", "` as the delimiter.

**2. Handling Empty Cells:** By setting `ignore_empty` to TRUE, you can ensure that no extra delimiters are added if some cells are empty.

**3. Combining with Other Functions:** You can use `TEXTJOIN` in conjunction with other functions, like `UPPER`, `LOWER`, or `MID`, to further manipulate text as you combine it.

**4. Large Ranges:** You can combine entire ranges without listing each cell. For instance, `=TEXTJOIN(", ", TRUE, A2:A10)` would combine all values from A2 to A10, separated by a comma and space.

# Function #49 - INDIRECT

The `INDIRECT` function in Excel returns a reference specified by a text string. This means you can use text to reference a cell or range, making your formulas more dynamic and adaptable. The primary benefits of the `INDIRECT` function include:

**1. Dynamic Referencing:** Easily change the reference of a formula without altering the formula itself.

**2. Drop-down Lists:** Combine with data validation to create dynamic drop-down lists that change based on other cell values.

**3. Variable Ranges:** Use in conjunction with other functions to create variable range references.

**4. Inter-Sheet Referencing:** Reference cells or ranges across different sheets dynamically.

---

**Step-by-Step Guide**

**Step 1:** Open your Excel workbook and navigate to the worksheet where you want to use the `INDIRECT` function.

**Step 2:** Click on the cell where you want the result to appear.

**Step 3:** Enter the `INDIRECT` function. The basic syntax for the function is:

---

### =INDIRECT(ref_text, [a1])

---

- `ref_text` is the text string that represents a cell or range reference.
- `a1` (optional) is a logical value that specifies the type of reference. If TRUE (or omitted), `ref_text` is interpreted as an A1-style reference. If FALSE, `ref_text` is interpreted as an R1C1-style reference.

> ➢ **Depending on your country, the ' , ' must be replaced by ' ; '**

**Step 4:** After entering the desired parameters, press `Enter`. Excel will display the value of the cell or range specified by the `ref_text`.

---

## Example

**Downloadable example:**
https://tinyurl.com/102-excel-functions

Imagine you have a workbook with monthly sales data on separate sheets named "January", "February", etc. On a summary sheet, you want to pull data for a specific month based on a cell input.

Data Setup:
- Sheets named "January", "February", etc., each with sales data in cell A1.
- On the summary sheet:

A1: Month (e.g., "January")
A2: Sales: ?

**Step 1:** Click on cell A2 on the summary sheet.

**Step 2:** Enter the `INDIRECT` function to pull the sales data based on the month specified in A1:

=INDIRECT(A1 & "!A1")

This formula constructs a reference by combining the month in A1 with the cell reference `!A1`.

**Step 3:** Press `Enter`. If A1 contains "January", Excel will display the sales data from cell A1 of the "January" sheet in A2 of the summary sheet.

**Step 4:** Change the month in A1 to "February" or any other month. A2 will dynamically update to show the sales data for the specified month.

> ## Advanced Tips:
>
> **1. Error Handling:** If `INDIRECT` references a non-existent cell or sheet, it will return a `#REF!` error. Ensure your references are valid.
>
> **2. Volatile Function:** `INDIRECT` is a volatile function, meaning it recalculates every time the worksheet recalculates, which can slow down large workbooks.
>
> **3. Combining with Other Functions:** `INDIRECT` can be combined with functions like `ROW`, `COLUMN`, `ADDRESS`, etc., to create more complex dynamic references.
>
> **4. R1C1 Reference Style:** By using the optional `[a1]` argument, you can switch between A1 and R1C1 reference styles. This can be useful for certain advanced applications.

# Function #50 - DATEDIF

The `DATEDIF` function calculates the difference between two dates in various units, such as days, months, or years. This function is particularly beneficial for:

**1. Age Calculation:** Easily determine the age of a person or the tenure of an employee.
**2. Project Management:** Calculate the duration of a project or time elapsed since the start.
**3. Financial Analysis:** Determine the maturity period of financial instruments.
**4. Event Planning:** Calculate days left for an upcoming event or anniversary.
**5. Inventory Management:** Determine the age of stock or time since the last inventory check.

---

### Step-by-Step Guide

**Step 1:** Open your Excel workbook and navigate to the worksheet where you want to use the `DATEDIF` function.

**Step 2:** Click on the cell where you want the result to appear.

**Step 3:** Enter the `DATEDIF` function. The syntax for the function is:

| =DATEDIF(start_date, end_date, unit) |
|---|

- `start_date` is the starting date.
- `end_date` is the ending date.
- `unit` specifies the time unit for the result (e.g., "D" for days, "M" for months, "Y" for years).

> ➤ **Depending on your country, the ' , ' must be replaced by ' ; '**

**Step 4:** After entering the desired parameters, press `Enter`. Excel will display the difference between the two dates based on the specified unit.

---

## Example

**Downloadable example:**
https://tinyurl.com/102-excel-functions

Scenario: Imagine you want to calculate the age of a person. You have their birthdate and today's date.

Data:

A1: Birthdate     B1: 15/01/1990
A2: Today         B2: =TODAY()
A3: Age           B3: ?

|   | A | B |
|---|---|---|
| 1 | Birthdate | 15/01/1990 |
| 2 | Today | =TODAY() |
| 3 | Age | |

**Step 1:** Click on cell B3.

**Step 2:** Enter the `DATEDIF` function to calculate the age:

=DATEDIF(B1, B2, "Y")

|   | A | B | C |
|---|---|---|---|
| 1 | Birthdate | 15/01/1990 | |
| 2 | Today | 23/08/2023 | |
| 3 | Age | =DATEDIF(B1; B2; "Y") | |

**Step 3:** Press `Enter`. Excel will display the age of the person in years in B3.

|   | A | B |
|---|---|---|
| 1 | Birthdate | 15/01/1990 |
| 2 | Today | 23/08/2023 |
| 3 | Age | 33 |

**Advanced Tips:**

**1. Other Units:** You can use different units in the `DATEDIF` function:
- "D" for days
- "M" for months
- "Y" for years
- "YM" for months excluding years
- "YD" for days excluding years
- "MD" for days excluding months and years

**2. Error Handling:** If `end_date` is earlier than `start_date`, `DATEDIF` will return a `#NUM!` error. Ensure your dates are in the correct order.

**3. Combining Units:** To get a more detailed age, like "X years, Y months," you can combine units:

   =DATEDIF(B1, B2, "Y") & " years, " & DATEDIF(B1, B2, "YM") & " months"

**4. Hidden Function:** Since `DATEDIF` isn't documented in some Excel versions, it might not appear in function suggestions. However, it works when entered correctly.

# Function #51 - ROUNDDOWN

The `ROUNDDOWN` function in Excel rounds a number down, towards zero, to a specified number of digits. This function is particularly beneficial for:

**1. Financial Calculations:** Ensure that estimations are conservative by always rounding down.

**2. Inventory Management:** Round down quantities to ensure you don't over-allocate.

**3. Data Analysis:** Standardize data points for easier comparison and analysis.

**4. Precision Control:** Ensure numbers are represented with a consistent level of detail.

**5. Reporting:** Display cleaner, more readable figures in reports and presentations.

---

## Step-by-Step Guide

**Step 1:** Open your Excel workbook and navigate to the worksheet where you want to use the `ROUNDDOWN` function.

**Step 2:** Click on the cell where you want the rounded result to appear.

**Step 3:** Enter the `ROUNDDOWN` function. The syntax for the function is:

| =ROUNDDOWN(number, num_digits) |
| --- |

- `number` is the value you want to round down.
- `num_digits` specifies the number of digits to which you want to round the `number`.

> ➢ **Depending on your country, the ' , ' must be replaced by ' ; '**

**Step 4:** After entering the desired parameters, press `Enter`. Excel will display the rounded number.

---

**Example**

**Downloadable example:**
https://tinyurl.com/102-excel-functions

Imagine you're calculating the price per unit of a product and want to ensure that you always round down to two decimal places to maintain a conservative estimate.

Data:

A1: Total Cost    B1: $123.4567
A2: Units        B2: 100
A3: Cost/Unit     B3: ?

| | A | B |
|---|---|---|
| 1 | Total Cost | 1234567 |
| 2 | Units | 100 |
| 3 | Cost/Unit | |

**Step 1:** Click on cell B3.

**Step 2:** Enter the `ROUNDDOWN` function to calculate the cost per unit and round it down to two decimal places:

=ROUNDDOWN(B1/B2, 2)

| | A | B | C | D |
|---|---|---|---|---|
| 1 | Total Cost | 1234567 | | |
| 2 | Units | 100 | | |
| 3 | Cost/Unit | =ROUNDDOWN(B1/B2; 2) | | |

**Step 3:** Press `Enter`. Excel will display the result `$1.23` in B3, rounding down the actual value of `$1.234567`.

| ▲ | A | B |
|---|---|---|
| 1 | Total Cost | 1234567 |
| 2 | Units | 100 |
| 3 | Cost/Unit | 12345,67 |
| 4 | | |

**Advanced Tips:**

**1. Rounding Whole Numbers:** If you use a negative number for `num_digits`, `ROUNDDOWN` will round down to the left of the decimal point. For example, `=ROUNDDOWN(123.4567, -1)` will return `120`.

**2. Difference with ROUND:** While both `ROUNDDOWN` and `ROUND` functions round numbers, `ROUNDDOWN` always rounds down, whereas `ROUND` rounds to the nearest number based on standard rounding rules.

**3. Combining with Other Functions**: You can use `ROUNDDOWN` in conjunction with other functions for more complex calculations. For instance, combining it with `SUM` or `AVERAGE` to round down the result of those functions.

# Function #52 - FIND

The `FIND` function in Excel is used to locate one text string within another text string and returns the starting position of the first text string from the first character of the second text string. The primary benefits of the `FIND` function include:

**1. Data Extraction:** Extract specific parts of text based on the position of certain characters or substrings.

**2. Text Analysis:** Determine if a specific substring exists within a larger string.

**3. Data Cleaning:** Identify and correct inconsistencies in datasets by locating specific characters or patterns.

**4. Case-Sensitive Searches:** Unlike the `SEARCH` function, `FIND` is case-sensitive, allowing for more precise text matching.

---

## Step-by-Step Guide

**Step 1:** Open your Excel workbook and navigate to the worksheet where you want to use the `FIND` function.

**Step 2:** Click on the cell where you want the result to appear.

**Step 3:** Enter the `FIND` function. The syntax for the function is:

---

**=FIND(find_text, within_text, [start_num])**

---

- `find_text` is the text you want to find.
- `within_text` is the text in which you want to search for `find_text`.
- `start_num` (optional) specifies the character at which to start the search. The first character in `within_text` is character number 1.

> ➤ **Depending on your country, the ' , ' must be replaced by ' ; '**

**Step 4:** After entering the desired parameters, press `Enter`. Excel will display the starting position of the `find_text` within the `within_text`.

---

**Example**

**Downloadable example:**
https://tinyurl.com/102-excel-functions

Imagine you have a list of email addresses, and you want to determine the position of the "@" symbol in each email to verify its presence.

Data:

A1: Email      B1: Position of "@"
A2: john.doe@email.com    B2: ?
A3: jane.smith@work.net   B3: ?

| | A | B | C |
|---|---|---|---|
| 1 | Email | Position of "@" | |
| 2 | john.doe@email.com | | |
| 3 | jane.smith@work.net | | |

**Step 1:** Click on cell B2.

**Step 2:** Enter the `FIND` function to locate the "@" symbol in the email address:

=FIND("@", A2)

| | A | B |
|---|---|---|
| 1 | Email | Position of "@" |
| 2 | john.doe@email.com | =FIND("@"; A2) |
| 3 | jane.smith@work.net | |
| 4 | | |

**Step 3:** Press `Enter`. Excel will display the result `9` in B2, indicating that the "@" symbol starts at the 9th character of the email address in A2.

| | A | B | C |
|---|---|---|---|
| 1 | Email | Position of "@" | |
| 2 | john.doe@email.com | 9 | |
| 3 | jane.smith@work.net | | |

**Step 4:** Drag the formula down in column B to apply it to the other email addresses. Cell B3 will display the position of the "@" symbol for the email address in A3.

| | A | B | C |
|---|---|---|---|
| 1 | Email | Position of "@" | |
| 2 | john.doe@email.com | 9 | |
| 3 | jane.smith@work.net | 11 | |
| 4 | | | |

**Advanced Tips:**

**1. Error Handling:** If `FIND` doesn't locate the `find_text`, it will return a `#VALUE!` error. You can use the `ISERROR` function to handle these errors gracefully.

**2. Case Sensitivity:** Remember that `FIND` is case-sensitive. If you need a case-insensitive search, consider using the `SEARCH` function.

**3. Combining with Other Functions:** You can use `FIND` in conjunction with functions like `LEFT`, `RIGHT`, or `MID` to extract specific parts of text based on the position of certain characters.

# Function #53 - SUMIF

The `SUMIF` function in Excel allows you to sum values based on a single condition. It's particularly beneficial for:

**1. Budgeting & Accounting:** Sum specific expenses or revenues based on categories or criteria.

**2. Inventory Management:** Calculate total quantities for specific items or categories.

**3. Data Analysis:** Aggregate data based on specific conditions or criteria.

**4. Reporting:** Generate summary reports by filtering and summing data based on certain conditions.

**5. Efficiency:** Avoid manual filtering or sorting, let `SUMIF` do the conditional summing for you.

---

## Step-by-Step Guide

**Step 1:** Open your Excel workbook and navigate to the worksheet where you want to use the `SUMIF` function.

**Step 2:** Click on the cell where you want the result to appear.

**Step 3:** Enter the `SUMIF` function. The syntax for the function is:

| =SUMIF(range, criteria, [sum_range]) |
|---|

- `range` is the range of cells you want to apply the criteria against.
- `criteria` is the condition you want to test the `range` against.
- `sum_range` (optional) is the actual cells to sum. If omitted, the cells in `range` are summed.

> ➤ **Depending on your country, the ' , ' must be replaced by ' ; '**

**Step 4:** After entering the desired parameters, press `Enter`. Excel will display the conditional sum based on the criteria.

---

**Example**

**Downloadable example:**
https://tinyurl.com/102-excel-functions

Imagine you have a list of sales transactions, and you want to determine the total sales for a specific product.

Data:

A1: Product      B1: Sales
A2: Apples       B2: $100
A3: Bananas      B3: $50
A4: Apples       B4: $150
A5: Oranges      B5: $80
A6: Total Sales for Apples:    B6: ?

| | A | B |
|---|---|---|
| 1 | Product | Sales |
| 2 | Apples | 100 |
| 3 | Bananas | 50 |
| 4 | Apples | 150 |
| 5 | Oranges | 80 |
| 6 | Total Sales for Apples | |

**Step 1:** Click on cell B6.

**Step 2:** Enter the `SUMIF` function to sum the sales for "Apples":

=SUMIF(A2:A5, "Apples", B2:B5)

| | A | B | C | D |
|---|---|---|---|---|
| 1 | Product | Sales | | |
| 2 | Apples | 100 | | |
| 3 | Bananas | 50 | | |
| 4 | Apples | 150 | | |
| 5 | Oranges | 80 | | |
| 6 | Total Sales for Apples | =SUMIF(A2:A5; "Apples"; B2:B5) | | |

**Step 3:** Press `Enter`. Excel will display the result `$250` in B6, indicating the total sales for "Apples".

| | A | B |
|---|---|---|
| 1 | Product | Sales |
| 2 | Apples | 100 |
| 3 | Bananas | 50 |
| 4 | Apples | 150 |
| 5 | Oranges | 80 |
| 6 | Total Sales for Apples | 250 |

---

**Advanced Tips:**

**1. Using Cell References:** Instead of hardcoding "Apples" in the formula, you can reference another cell. For example, if A6 contains "Apples", the formula would be `=SUMIF(A2:A5, A6, B2:B5)`.

**2. Multiple Conditions:** If you need to sum based on multiple conditions, consider using the `SUMIFS` function, which allows for multiple criteria.

**3. Non-Numeric Criteria:** You can use operators in your criteria, such as `">100"` to sum values greater than 100.

**4. Wildcards:** The `SUMIF` function supports wildcards like `*` and `?`. For instance, `"A*"` would match any value in the range starting with the letter "A".

---

# Function #54 - CONCATENATE

The `CONCATENATE` function in Excel is used to join two or more text strings into one string. It's especially beneficial for:

**1. Data Cleaning & Preparation:** Combine data from multiple columns into a single column.

**2. Generating Unique Identifiers:** Create IDs or codes by combining various data elements.

**3. Formatting Output:** Prepare data for reports, presentations, or other applications by combining text in a specific format.

**4. Enhancing Data Analysis:** Combine text values to create new categories or labels for analysis.

**5. Simplifying Complex Formulas:** Use `CONCATENATE` to build complex strings in a more readable manner.

---

## Step-by-Step Guide

**Step 1:** Open your Excel workbook and navigate to the worksheet where you want to use the `CONCATENATE` function.

**Step 2:** Click on the cell where you want the combined text to appear.

**Step 3:** Enter the `CONCATENATE` function. The syntax for the function is:

---

**=CONCATENATE(text1, [text2], ...)**

---

- `text1, text2, ...` are the text items you want to join. You can specify up to 255 text arguments.

➤ **Depending on your country, the ' , ' must be replaced by ' ; '**

**Step 4:** After entering the desired text strings or cell references, press `Enter`. Excel will display the combined text.

---

**Example**

**Downloadable example:**
https://tinyurl.com/102-excel-functions

Imagine you have a list of first names and last names, and you want to create a full name column.

Data:

A1: First Name     B1: Last Name     C1: Full Name

A2: John      B2: Doe      C2: ?
A3: Jane      B3: Smith      C3: ?

| | A | B | C |
|---|---|---|---|
| 1 | First Name | Last Name | Full Name |
| 2 | John | Doe | |
| 3 | Jane | Smith | |

**Step 1:** Click on cell C2.

**Step 2:** Enter the `CONCATENATE` function to combine the first name and last name:

=CONCATENATE(A2, " ", B2)

| | A | B | C | D | E |
|---|---|---|---|---|---|
| 1 | First Name | Last Name | Full Name | | |
| 2 | John | Doe | =CONCATENATE(A2; " "; B2) | | |
| 3 | Jane | Smith | | | |

Note the use of `" "` to insert a space between the first name and last name.

**Step 3:** Press `Enter`. Excel will display the result `John Doe` in C2.

| | A | B | C |
|---|---|---|---|
| 1 | First Name | Last Name | Full Name |
| 2 | John | Doe | John Doe |
| 3 | Jane | Smith | |

**Step 4:** Drag the formula down in column C to apply it to the other names. Cell C3 will display `Jane Smith`.

| ◢ | A | B | C |
|---|---|---|---|
| 1 | First Name | Last Name | Full Name |
| 2 | John | Doe | John Doe |
| 3 | Jane | Smith | Jane Smith |

---

**Advanced Tips:**

**1. Using & Operator:** Instead of `CONCATENATE`, you can use the `&` operator to join text. The formula `=A2 & " " & B2` would produce the same result as the example above.

**2. Newer CONCAT Function:** In newer versions of Excel, there's a `CONCAT` function that provides similar functionality to `CONCATENATE` but can handle a range of cells, making it more versatile.

**3. Dynamic Data:** Remember, if the data in the referenced cells changes, the result of the `CONCATENATE` function will update automatically.

---

# Function #55 - TRANSPOSE

The `TRANSPOSE` function in Excel allows you to switch the rows and columns with each other, essentially rotating your data. This function is particularly beneficial for:

**1. Data Presentation:** Adjust data layout to fit specific reporting formats or visual preferences.

**2. Optimizing Data Analysis:** Some data analysis tools or techniques may require data in a specific orientation.

**3. Space Management:** In cases where horizontal space is limited, transposing can make data more readable by presenting it vertically.

**4. Data Import/Export:** Adjust data structures to meet the requirements of external systems or software.

---

## Step-by-Step Guide

**Step 1:** Open your Excel workbook and navigate to the worksheet containing the data you want to transpose.

**Step 2:** Identify the range of cells you want to transpose. Note the number of rows and columns in this range.

**Step 3:** Select a new area in the worksheet where you want the transposed data to appear. This area should have a number of rows equal to the number of columns in the original range, and vice versa.

**Step 4:** Without clicking anywhere else, type the `TRANSPOSE` function:

---

## =TRANSPOSE(reference)

---

Where `reference` is the range of cells you want to transpose.

**Step 5:** Instead of pressing `Enter`, press `Ctrl + Shift + Enter`. This turns your function into an array formula, and Excel will transpose the data into the selected area.

---

### Example

Imagine you have a dataset of monthly sales figures, presented in a horizontal format, and you want to transpose them into a vertical format.

Data:

A1: January   B1: February   C1: March
A2: $5,000    B2: $6,000     C2: $5,500

| ◢ | A | B | C | D |
|---|---|---|---|---|
| 1 | January | February | March | |
| 2 | 5000 | 6000 | 5500 | |
| 3 | | | | |

**Step 1:** Select an empty area in the worksheet that has 3 rows and 2 columns (since we're transposing a 2x3 range to a 3x2 range).

**Step 2:** Without clicking anywhere else, type the formula:

=TRANSPOSE(A1:C2)

| ◢ | A | B | C | D | E | F |
|---|---|---|---|---|---|---|
| 1 | January | February | March | | =TRANSPOSE(A1:C2) | |
| 2 | 5000 | 6000 | 5500 | | February | 6000 |
| 3 | | | | | March | 5500 |

**Step 3:** Press `Ctrl + Shift + Enter`. The selected area will now display:

A4: January   B4: $5,000
A5: February  B5: $6,000
A6: March     B6: $5,500

| | A | B | C | D | E | F |
|---|---|---|---|---|---|---|
| 1 | January | February | March | | January | 5000 |
| 2 | 5000 | 6000 | 5500 | | February | 6000 |
| 3 | | | | | March | 5500 |
| 4 | | | | | | |

---

**Advanced Tips:**

**1. Dynamic Arrays:** In the latest versions of Excel, the `TRANSPOSE` function supports dynamic arrays. This means you can simply enter the formula and press `Enter` (no need for `Ctrl + Shift + Enter`), and Excel will automatically spill the transposed data into the necessary cells.

**2. Editing Transposed Data:** Remember, the transposed data is linked to the original data. If you change a value in the transposed range, the original data will also change, and vice versa.

**3. Array Limitations:** Since the `TRANSPOSE` function creates an array formula, you can't edit individual cells within the transposed range without breaking the array. To edit individual values, you'd need to break the array link or edit the original data.

---

# Function #56 - MATCH

The `MATCH` function in Excel searches for a specified item in a range of cells and then returns the relative position of that item within the range. The primary benefits of the `MATCH` function include:

**1. Lookup Operations:** Find the position of specific data within a list or table.

**2. Dynamic Referencing:** Use in combination with other functions like `INDEX` to create dynamic lookup formulas.

**3. Data Validation:** Check if a particular value exists within a dataset and where it's located.

**4. Flexibility:** Works with both vertical and horizontal ranges.

**5. Error Handling:** Easily identify if a value doesn't exist in a given range.

---

**Step-by-Step Guide**

**Step 1:** Open your Excel workbook and navigate to the worksheet where you want to use the `MATCH` function.

Step 2: Click on the cell where you want the result to appear.

**Step 3:** Enter the `MATCH` function. The syntax for the function is:

> =MATCH(lookup_value, lookup_array,
> [match_type])

- `lookup_value` is the value you want to search for.
- `lookup_array` is the range of cells containing the data.
- `match_type` (optional) specifies how Excel matches the `lookup_value` with values in `lookup_array`. It can be 1 (less than), 0 (exact match), or -1 (greater than).

➤ **Depending on your country, the ' , ' must be replaced by ' ; '**

**Step 4:** After entering the desired parameters, press `Enter`. Excel will display the relative position of the `lookup_value` within the `lookup_array`.

---

**Example**

**Downloadable example:**
https://tinyurl.com/102-excel-functions

Imagine you have a list of products and their prices. You want to find out the position of a specific product in the list.

Data:

A1: Product     B1: Price
A2: Apples     B2: $1.00
A3: Bananas     B3: $0.75
A4: Cherries     B4: $2.50
A5: Position of Bananas:    B5: ?

| | A | B |
|---|---|---|
| 1 | Product | Price |
| 2 | Apples | 1 |
| 3 | Bananas | 0,75 |
| 4 | Cherries | 2,5 |
| 5 | Position of Bananas | |
| 6 | | |

**Step 1:** Click on cell B5.

**Step 2:** Enter the `MATCH` function to find the position of "Bananas" in the product list:

=MATCH("Bananas", A2:A4, 0)

| | A | B | C |
|---|---|---|---|
| 1 | Product | Price | |
| 2 | Apples | 1 | |
| 3 | Bananas | 0,75 | |
| 4 | Cherries | 2,5 | |
| 5 | Position of Bananas | =MATCH("Bananas";A2:A4; 0) | |

**Step 3:** Press `Enter`. Excel will display the result `2` in B5, indicating that "Bananas" is the second item in the product list.

| | A | B |
|---|---|---|
| 1 | Product | Price |
| 2 | Apples | 1 |
| 3 | Bananas | 0,75 |
| 4 | Cherries | 2,5 |
| 5 | Position of Bananas | 2 |

**Advanced Tips:**

**1. Using with INDEX:** The `MATCH` function is often used with the `INDEX` function to retrieve a value at a specific position in a range. For example, `INDEX(B2:B4, MATCH("Bananas", A2:A4, 0))` would return the price of Bananas.

**2. Handling Errors:** If `MATCH` doesn't find the `lookup_value`, it will return a `#N/A` error. You can use functions like `IFERROR` to handle these gracefully.

**3. Approximate Match:** By using a `match_type` of 1 or -1, you can find the largest value less than or equal to `lookup_value` or the smallest value greater than or equal to `lookup_value`, respectively. Ensure your `lookup_array` is sorted appropriately for these options.

## Function #57 - ISERROR

The `ISERROR` function in Excel checks whether a value is an error (`#N/A`, `#VALUE!`, `#REF!`, `#DIV/0!`, `#NUM!`, `#NAME?`, or `#NULL!`) and returns `TRUE` if it is an error and `FALSE` if it isn't. The primary benefits of the `ISERROR` function include:

**1. Error Handling:** Identify cells that contain error values and handle them appropriately.

**2. Data Cleaning:** Ensure that data sets are free from errors before performing further analysis.

**3. Enhanced User Experience:** Replace error messages with user-friendly messages or alternative values.

**4. Conditional Formatting:** Highlight or format cells that contain errors.

**5. Data Validation:** Prevent formulas from breaking due to errors in input cells.

---

### Step-by-Step Guide

**Step 1:** Open your Excel workbook and navigate to the worksheet where you want to use the `ISERROR` function.

**Step 2:** Click on the cell where you want the result to appear.

**Step 3:** Enter the `ISERROR` function. The syntax for the function is:

| =ISERROR(value) |
|---|

- `value` is the expression or cell reference you want to test for an error.

**Step 4:** After entering the desired parameters, press `Enter`. Excel will display `TRUE` if the value is an error and `FALSE` otherwise.

---

**Example**

**Downloadable example:**
https://tinyurl.com/102-excel-functions

Imagine you have a dataset where you're dividing numbers. You want to identify cells where a division error occurs (e.g., division by zero).

Data:

A1: Number    B1: Divider    C1: Result    D1: Contains Error?

A2: 10    B2: 5    C2: =A2/B2    D2: ?
A3: 20    B3: 0    C3: =A3/B3    D3: ?

| | A | B | C | D |
|---|---|---|---|---|
| 1 | Number | Divider | Result | Contains Error? |
| 2 | 10 | 5 | 2 | |
| 3 | 20 | 0 | #DIV/0! | |

**Step 1:** Click on cell D2.

**Step 2:** Enter the `ISERROR` function to check if the result in C2 contains an error:

=ISERROR(C2)

| | A | B | C | D |
|---|---|---|---|---|
| 1 | Number | Divider | Result | Contains Error? |
| 2 | 10 | 5 | 2 | =ISERROR(C2) |
| 3 | 20 | 0 | #DIV/0! | |

**Step 3:** Press `Enter`. Excel will display `FALSE` in D2, indicating that there's no error in C2.

Step 4: Drag the formula from D2 to D3. Cell D3 will display `TRUE`, indicating that there's an error in C3 (since we're trying to divide by zero).

| | A | B | C | D |
|---|---|---|---|---|
| 1 | Number | Divider | Result | Contains Error? |
| 2 | 10 | 5 | 2 | FALSE |
| 3 | 20 | 0 | #DIV/0! | TRUE |

**Advanced Tips:**

**1. Using with IF:** Combine `ISERROR` with the `IF` function to replace error values. For example, `=IF(ISERROR(C2), "Error", C2)` would display "Error" if C2 contains an error and the actual value of C2 otherwise.

**2. Other Error Functions:** Excel also offers `ISERR` (checks for all errors except `#N/A`) and `IFERROR` (returns a value you specify if an error is found, otherwise returns the formula's result).

**3. Error Types:** Familiarize yourself with common Excel errors so you can better understand and troubleshoot them when they arise.

# Function #58 - ISFORMULA

The `ISFORMULA` function in Excel checks whether a cell contains a formula and returns `TRUE` if it does, and `FALSE` if it doesn't. The primary benefits of the `ISFORMULA` function include:

**1. Formula Auditing:** Quickly identify which cells in a worksheet contain formulas.

**2. Data Validation:** Ensure that certain cells contain formulas as expected.

**3. Enhanced User Experience:** Provide feedback or conditional formatting based on the presence of formulas.

**4. Error Prevention:** Detect cells that should contain formulas but have been overwritten with static values.

---

### Step-by-Step Guide

**Step 1:** Open your Excel workbook and navigate to the worksheet where you want to use the `ISFORMULA` function.

**Step 2:** Click on the cell where you want the result to appear.

**Step 3:** Enter the `ISFORMULA` function. The syntax for the function is:

| =ISFORMULA(reference) |
| --- |

- `reference` is the cell you want to check for a formula.

**Step 4:** After entering the desired parameters, press `Enter`. Excel will display `TRUE` if the referenced cell contains a formula and `FALSE` otherwise.

---

**Example**

**Downloadable example:**
https://tinyurl.com/102-excel-functions

Imagine you have a dataset where you've calculated the sales tax for various items. You want to ensure that all tax values were calculated using a formula.

Data:

A1: Item     B1: Price     C1: Sales Tax (10%)     D1: Contains Formula?
A2: Apple     B2: $1.00     C2: =B2*0.10       D2: ?
A3: Banana     B3: $0.50     C3: $0.05       D3: ?

| | A | B | C | D |
|---|---|---|---|---|
| 1 | Item | Price | Sales Tax (10%) | Contains Formula? |
| 2 | Apple | 1 | 0,1 | |
| 3 | Banana | 0,5 | 0,05 | |
| 4 | | | | |

**Step 1:** Click on cell D2.

**Step 2:** Enter the `ISFORMULA` function to check if the sales tax in C2 was calculated using a formula:

=ISFORMULA(C2)

| | A | B | C | D |
|---|---|---|---|---|
| 1 | Item | Price | Sales Tax (10%) | Contains Formula? |
| 2 | Apple | 1 | 0,1 | =ISFORMULA(C2) |
| 3 | Banana | 0,5 | 0,05 | |

**Step 3:** Press `Enter`. Excel will display `TRUE` in D2, indicating that C2 contains a formula.

| | A | B | C | D |
|---|---|---|---|---|
| 1 | Item | Price | Sales Tax (10%) | Contains Formula? |
| 2 | Apple | 1 | 0,1 | TRUE |
| 3 | Banana | 0,5 | 0,05 | |

**Step 4:** Drag the formula from D2 to D3. Cell D3 will display `FALSE`, indicating that C3 does not contain a formula (it has a static value).

| | A | B | C | D |
|---|---|---|---|---|
| 1 | Item | Price | Sales Tax (10%) | Contains Formula? |
| 2 | Apple | 1 | 0,1 | TRUE |
| 3 | Banana | 0,5 | 0,05 | FALSE |

**Advanced Tips:**

**1. Using with Conditional Formatting:** You can use the `ISFORMULA` function with conditional formatting to highlight cells that contain formulas. This is useful for visually auditing large worksheets.

**2. Combining with Other Functions:** Combine `ISFORMULA` with functions like `IF` to create more complex logic. For example, `=IF(ISFORMULA(C2), "Calculated", "Static")` would display "Calculated" if C2 contains a formula and "Static" otherwise.

**3. Auditing Large Ranges:** If you want to check a large range for formulas, you can copy the `ISFORMULA` function down a column to quickly see which cells in the adjacent column contain formulas.

# Function #59 - AGGREGATE

The `AGGREGATE` function in Excel provides the functionality of 19 different functions, including some that are not available as standalone functions in Excel. It can perform calculations like SUM, AVERAGE, COUNT, etc., while allowing you to ignore errors, hidden rows, or other specific conditions.

Primary benefits of the `AGGREGATE` function include:

**1. Versatility:** Combines the functionality of multiple functions into one.

**2. Error Handling:** Can easily bypass errors in the dataset.

**3. Flexibility:** Can ignore hidden rows, nested SUBTOTAL and AGGREGATE functions, or filter data with criteria.

**4. Enhanced Calculations:** Useful for datasets that might have errors or need specific conditions to be ignored.

---

**Step-by-Step Guide**

**Step 1:** Open your Excel workbook and navigate to the worksheet where you want to use the `AGGREGATE` function.

**Step 2:** Click on the cell where you want the result to appear.

**Step 3:** Enter the `AGGREGATE` function. The syntax for the function is:

| =AGGREGATE(function_num, options, array, [k]) |
|---|

- `function_num` is a number representing the function you want to use (e.g., 1 for AVERAGE, 9 for SUM).
- `options` is a number representing which values or errors you want to ignore.
- `array` is the range of cells you want to aggregate.
- `[k]` is an optional parameter used for functions that require a k value, like SMALL or LARGE.

> **Depending on your country, the ' , ' must be replaced by ' ; '**

**Step 4:** After entering the desired parameters, press `Enter`.

**Example**

**Downloadable example:**
https://tinyurl.com/102-excel-functions

Imagine you have a dataset of sales figures. Some cells contain errors (`#DIV/0!`), and you want to find the average of the sales figures while ignoring these errors.

Data:

A1: Sales
A2: 100
A3: 200
A4: #DIV/0!
A5: 300
A6: Average Sales:    B6: ?

| | A |
|---|---|
| 1 | Sales |
| 2 | 100 |
| 3 | 200 |
| 4 | #DIV/0! |
| 5 | 300 |
| 6 | Average Sales: |

**Step 1:** Click on cell B6.

**Step 2:** Enter the `AGGREGATE` function to calculate the average while ignoring errors:

## =AGGREGATE(1, 6, A2:A5)

| | A | B | C |
|---|---|---|---|
| 1 | Sales | | |
| 2 | 100 | | |
| 3 | 200 | | |
| 4 | #DIV/0! | | |
| 5 | 300 | | |
| 6 | Average Sales: | =AGGREGATE(1; 6; A2:A5) | |
| 7 | | | |

Here, `1` represents the AVERAGE function, and `6` tells Excel to ignore error values.

**Step 3:** Press `Enter`. Excel will display the average of the sales figures in B6, ignoring the error in A4.

| | A | B |
|---|---|---|
| 1 | Sales | |
| 2 | 100 | |
| 3 | 200 | |
| 4 | #DIV/0! | |
| 5 | 300 | |
| 6 | Average Sales: | 200 |
| 7 | | |

**Advanced Tips:**

**1. Using with Arrays:** The `AGGREGATE` function can handle arrays, making it powerful for more complex operations.

**2. Combining Options:** You can combine options by adding their numbers together. For example, to ignore hidden rows (option 5) and error values (option 6), use `11` as the option value.

**3. Filtering with Criteria:** For functions 14 to 19, you can use criteria to filter the data you're aggregating, similar to the `SUMIF` or `AVERAGEIF` functions.

# Function #60 - CHAR

The `CHAR` function in Excel returns the character specified by a number (from 1 to 255) in the ASCII table. It's the inverse of the `CODE` function, which gives the ASCII value of a character.

Primary benefits of the `CHAR` function include:

**1. Data Formatting:** Useful for adding specific characters, like line breaks or tabs, within cells.

**2. Data Representation:** Convert ASCII values to their corresponding characters.

**3. Custom Text Functions:** Create custom text functions by combining `CHAR` with other text functions.

---

## Step-by-Step Guide

**Step 1:** Open your Excel workbook and navigate to the worksheet where you want to use the `CHAR` function.

**Step 2:** Click on the cell where you want the character to appear.

**Step 3:** Enter the `CHAR` function. The syntax for the function is:

| =CHAR(number) |
|---|

- `number` is the ASCII value of the character you want to retrieve.

**Step 4:** After entering the desired number, press `Enter`.

---

## Example

**Downloadable example:**
https://tinyurl.com/102-excel-functions

Imagine you're creating a list and want to separate items with a line break within a single cell.

Data:

A1: Apple
A2: Banana
A3: Combined:    B3: ?

| | A |
|---|---|
| 1 | Apple |
| 2 | Banana |
| 3 | Combined |

**Step 1:** Click on cell B3.

**Step 2:** Enter the formula to combine the items in A1 and A2 with a line break:

=A1 & CHAR(10) & A2

Here, `CHAR(10)` represents a line break in Excel.

| | A | B |
|---|---|---|
| 1 | Apple | |
| 2 | Banana | |
| 3 | Combined | =A1 & CHAR(10) & A2 |

**Step 3:** Press `Enter`. Cell B3 will display "Apple" and "Banana" separated by a line break.

| | A | B |
|---|---|---|
| 1 | Apple | |
| 2 | Banana | |
| 3 | Combined | Apple Banana |

**Note:** For the line break to be visible, you'll need to have "Wrap Text" enabled for cell B3.

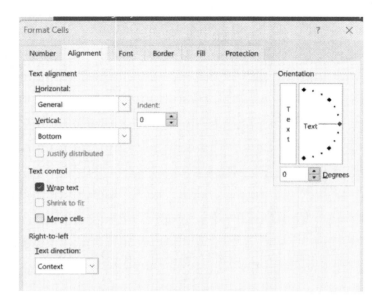

**Advanced Tips:**

**1. Special Characters:** Some commonly used ASCII values with `CHAR` are 10 (line break), 9 (tab), and 34 (double quotation mark).

**2. Combining with Other Functions:** You can combine `CHAR` with functions like `MID`, `LEFT`, and `RIGHT` to manipulate text in creative ways.

**3. Understanding ASCII:** Familiarize yourself with the ASCII table to know which numbers correspond to which characters. This will help you use the `CHAR` function more effectively.

# Function #61 - TEXT

The `TEXT` function in Excel converts a numeric value to text and lets you specify the display formatting by using special format strings. This is particularly useful when you want to display numbers in a more readable or customized format without changing the actual number value.

Primary benefits of the `TEXT` function include:

**1. Custom Formatting:** Display numbers in various formats like currency, percentages, dates, and more.
**2. Data Presentation:** Make data more reader-friendly or adhere to specific reporting standards.
**3. Combining Text and Numbers:** Seamlessly integrate numbers within textual content.

---

## Step-by-Step Guide

**Step 1:** Open your Excel workbook and navigate to the worksheet where you want to use the `TEXT` function.

**Step 2:** Click on the cell where you want the formatted text to appear.

**Step 3:** Enter the `TEXT` function. The syntax for the function is:

| =TEXT(value, format_text) |
|:-:|

- `value` is the numeric value you want to format.
- `format_text` is the format in which you want to display the number.

**Step 4:** After entering the desired parameters, press `Enter`.

---

**Example**

**Downloadable example:**
https://tinyurl.com/102-excel-functions

Scenario: Imagine you're preparing a report and want to display sales figures in a currency format and dates in a specific style.

Data:

A1: Sales Amount:    B1: 5000
A2: Sale Date:       B2: 44544 (This is an Excel date serial number for 1st Jan 2022)
A3: Formatted Sales: B3: ?
A4: Formatted Date:  B4: ?

| | A | B |
|---|---|---|
| 1 | Sales Amount: | 5000 |
| 2 | Sale Date: | 44544 |
| 3 | Formatted Sales | |
| 4 | Formatted Date: | |

**Step 1:** Click on cell B3.

**Step 2:** Enter the formula to format the sales amount in B1 as currency:

=TEXT(B1, "$#,##0.00")

**Step 3:** Press `Enter`. Cell B3 will display "$5,000.00".

**Step 4:** Click on cell B4.

**Step 5:** Enter the formula to format the date in B2:

=TEXT(B2, "dd-mmm-yyyy")

**Step 6:** Press `Enter`. Cell B4 will display "01-Jan-2022".

**Advanced Tips:**

**1. Understanding Format Codes:** Familiarize yourself with various format codes like "dd" for day, "mm" for month, "yyyy" for year, etc., to customize your formatting.

**2. Combining with Other Functions:** You can combine `TEXT` with functions like `CONCATENATE` or `&` to create custom strings that integrate numbers and text.

**3. Locale-Specific Formatting:** The `TEXT` function's formatting might vary based on your system's locale settings. Ensure you're using the correct format strings for your locale.

# Function #62 - MAXIFS

The `MAXIFS` function in Excel returns the maximum value among cells within a range based on multiple criteria. It's an extension of the `MAX` function, but with the added capability to filter data based on specific conditions.

Primary benefits of the `MAXIFS` function include:

**1. Data Filtering:** Easily find the maximum value in a dataset based on specific criteria.

**2. Multiple Criteria:** Unlike `MAXIF`, `MAXIFS` can handle multiple conditions, providing more flexibility.

**3. Data Analysis:** Quickly analyze datasets to find the highest value under certain conditions without sorting or manually filtering data.

---

**Step-by-Step Guide**

**Step 1:** Open your Excel workbook and navigate to the worksheet where you want to use the `MAXIFS` function.

**Step 2:** Click on the cell where you want the result to appear.

**Step 3:** Enter the `MAXIFS` function. The syntax for the function is:

| =MAXIFS(max_range, criteria_range1, criteria1, [criteria_range2, criteria2], ...) |
| --- |

- `max_range` is the range of cells from which you want to find the maximum value.
- `criteria_range1` is the range of cells you want to evaluate with the first condition.
- `criteria1` is the condition for the first criteria range.
- Additional criteria ranges and conditions can be added as needed.

> ➢ **Depending on your country, the ' , ' must be replaced by ' ; '**

**Step 4:** After entering the desired parameters, press `Enter`.

**Example**

**Downloadable example:**
https://tinyurl.com/102-excel-functions

Imagine you have a dataset of sales figures for different products and regions. You want to find the highest sales figure for a specific product in a specific region.

Data:

A1: Product    B1: Region    C1: Sales
A2: Apple     B2: North    C2: 100
A3: Banana    B3: South    C3: 150
A4: Apple     B4: South    C4: 200
A5: Banana    B5: North    C5: 50
A6: Highest Sales for Apple in South:    B6: ?

| | A | B | C |
|---|---|---|---|
| 1 | Product | Region | Sales |
| 2 | Apple | North | 100 |
| 3 | Banana | South | 150 |
| 4 | Apple | South | 200 |
| 5 | Banana | North | 50 |
| 6 | Highest Sales for Apple in South: | | |

**Step 1:** Click on cell B6.

**Step 2:** Enter the formula to find the highest sales for the product "Apple" in the "South" region:

=MAXIFS(C2:C5, A2:A5, "Apple", B2:B5, "South")

**Step 3:** Press `Enter`. Cell B6 will display "200", which is the highest sales figure for Apple in the South region.

---

**Advanced Tips:**

**1. Using Cell References:** Instead of hardcoding criteria like "Apple" or "South", you can use cell references to make the function more dynamic.

**2. Combining with Other Functions:** You can combine `MAXIFS` with functions like `MINIFS` to create more complex data analyses.

**3. Understanding Criteria:** Ensure that criteria are correctly specified. For example, use `">100"` to filter values greater than 100.

---

# Function #63 - HOUR

The `HOUR` function in Excel is used to extract the hour component from a time value. The function returns an integer representing the hour, ranging from 0 (12:00 AM) to 23 (11:00 PM).

Primary benefits of the `HOUR` function include:

**1. Time Decomposition:** Break down time values to analyze or format them separately.

**2. Data Analysis:** Useful in scenarios where you need to categorize or filter data based on specific hours of the day.

**3. Time Calculations:** Combine with other time functions to perform complex time-related computations.

---

## Step-by-Step Guide

**Step 1:** Open your Excel workbook and navigate to the worksheet where you want to use the `HOUR` function.

**Step 2:** Click on the cell where you want the extracted hour to appear.

**Step 3:** Enter the `HOUR` function. The syntax for the function is:

| **=HOUR(serial_number)** |
|:---:|

- `serial_number` is the Excel time from which you want to extract the hour.

**Step 4:** After entering the desired time value or cell reference, press `Enter`.

---

**Example**

**Downloadable example:**
https://tinyurl.com/102-excel-functions

Imagine you have a dataset of timestamps for various events, and you want to extract the hour when each event occurred.

Data:

A1: Timestamp          B1: Event Hour
A2: 2023-08-16 15:45   B2: ?
A3: 2023-08-16 08:30   B3: ?
A4: 2023-08-16 20:15   B4: ?

| | A | B |
|---|---|---|
| 1 | Timestamp | Event Hour |
| 2 | 16/08/2023 15:45 | |
| 3 | 16/08/2023 08:30 | |
| 4 | 16/08/2023 20:15 | |

**Step 1:** Click on cell B2.

**Step 2:** Enter the formula to extract the hour from the timestamp in A2:

=HOUR(A2)

| | A | B |
|---|---|---|
| 1 | Timestamp | Event Hour |
| 2 | 16/08/2023 15:45 | =HOUR(A2) |
| 3 | 16/08/2023 08:30 | |
| 4 | 16/08/2023 20:15 | |
| 5 | | |

**Step 3:** Press `Enter`. Cell B2 will display "15", representing the 15th hour or 3:00 PM.

| | A | B |
|---|---|---|
| 1 | Timestamp | Event Hour |
| 2 | 16/08/2023 15:45 | 15 |
| 3 | 16/08/2023 08:30 | |
| 4 | 16/08/2023 20:15 | |

**Step 4:** Drag the formula from B2 down to B4 to fill the remaining cells. Cells B3 and B4 will display "8" and "20", respectively.

| | A | B | |
|---|---|---|---|
| 1 | Timestamp | Event Hour | |
| 2 | 16/08/2023 15:45 | 15 | |
| 3 | 16/08/2023 08:30 | 8 | |
| 4 | 16/08/2023 20:15 | 20 | |

**Advanced Tips:**

**1. Using with Other Functions:** Combine `HOUR` with `MINUTE` and `SECOND` functions to fully decompose a time value.

**2. Time Formatting:** Ensure that the cells containing time values are correctly formatted as Date or Time in Excel.

**3. 24-Hour Format:** Remember that `HOUR` returns values in a 24-hour format. If you need a 12-hour format, you'll need to make additional adjustments.

# Function #64 - ISNUMBER

The `ISNUMBER` function in Excel is used to determine if a cell contains a number or not. It returns `TRUE` if the cell contains a number and `FALSE` otherwise.

Primary benefits of the `ISNUMBER` function include:

**1. Data Validation:** Ensure that data entered or imported into Excel meets specific criteria, such as being numeric.

**2. Error Handling:** Identify cells that might cause errors in calculations due to non-numeric content.

**3. Data Cleaning:** Assist in the process of cleaning and preparing data for analysis.

---

**Step-by-Step Guide**

**Step 1:** Open your Excel workbook and navigate to the worksheet where you want to use the `ISNUMBER` function.

**Step 2:** Click on the cell where you want the result (TRUE or FALSE) to appear.

**Step 3:** Enter the `ISNUMBER` function. The syntax for the function is:

---

### =ISNUMBER(value)

---

- `value` is the cell or value you want to test.

**Step 4:** After entering the desired cell reference or value, press `Enter`.

---

### Example

### Downloadable example:
https://tinyurl.com/102-excel-functions

Imagine you have a dataset of various entries, and you want to determine which of them are numbers.

Data:

```
A1: Entry      B1: Is Number?
A2: 123        B2: ?
A3: Apple      B3: ?
A4: 45.67      B4: ?
A5: #VALUE!    B5: ?
```

| | A | B |
|---|---|---|
| 1 | Entry | Is Number |
| 2 | 123 | |
| 3 | Apple | |
| 4 | 45.67 | |
| 5 | #VALUE! | |

**Step 1:** Click on cell B2.

**Step 2:** Enter the formula to check if the entry in A2 is a number:

=ISNUMBER(A2)

| | A | B |
|---|---|---|
| 1 | Entry | Is Number |
| 2 | 123 | =ISNUMBER(A2) |
| 3 | Apple | |
| 4 | 45.67 | |
| 5 | #VALUE! | |

**Step 3:** Press `Enter`. Cell B2 will display `TRUE` since 123 is a number.

| | A | B |
|---|---|---|
| 1 | Entry | Is Number |
| 2 | 123 | TRUE |
| 3 | Apple | |
| 4 | 45.67 | |
| 5 | #VALUE! | |
| 6 | | |

**Step 4:** Drag the formula from B2 down to B5 to fill the remaining cells. Cells B3, B4, and B5 will display `FALSE`, `TRUE`, and `FALSE`, respectively.

| | A | B |
|---|---|---|
| 1 | Entry | Is Number |
| 2 | 123 | TRUE |
| 3 | Apple | FALSE |
| 4 | 45,67 | TRUE |
| 5 | #VALUE! | FALSE |

---

**Advanced Tips:**

**1. Combining with Other Functions:** You can combine `ISNUMBER` with functions like `SEARCH` to find if a text string contains a number.

**2. Handling Errors:** Use `ISNUMBER` in conjunction with the `IF` function to provide custom outputs or messages for non-numeric values.

**3. Data Types:** Remember that `ISNUMBER` only checks for numeric data types. It will return `FALSE` for numeric text strings unless combined with other functions.

---

# Function #65 - TRIM

The `TRIM` function in Excel is used to remove extra spaces from a text string, leaving only single spaces between words and no space characters at the start or end of the text.

Primary benefits of the `TRIM` function include:

1. **Data Cleaning:** Essential for preparing data for analysis, especially if it's been imported from external sources that might have inconsistent spacing.
2. **Improving Accuracy:** Prevents potential lookup errors or mismatches caused by extra spaces.
3. **Enhancing Presentation:** Makes data look cleaner and more professional.

**Step-by-Step Guide**

**Step 1:** Open your Excel workbook and navigate to the worksheet where you want to use the `TRIM` function.

**Step 2:** Click on the cell where you want the trimmed text to appear.

**Step 3:** Enter the `TRIM` function. The syntax for the function is:

| =TRIM(text) |
|:---:|

- `text` is the cell or text string you want to trim.

**Step 4:** After entering the desired cell reference or text string, press `Enter`.

---

**Example**

**Downloadable example:**
https://tinyurl.com/102-excel-functions

Imagine you have a dataset of product names, but they've been entered inconsistently with extra spaces.

Data:

A1: Product Name      B1: Trimmed Name
A2: "  Apple  "      B2: ?
A3: "Banana  "      B3: ?
A4: "  Cherry  Pie  "      B4: ?

| | A |
|---|---|
| 1 | Product Name |
| 2 | " Apple " |
| 3 | "Banana " |
| 4 | " Cherry Pie " |

**Step 1:** Click on cell B2.

**Step 2:** Enter the formula to trim the product name in A2:

=TRIM(A2)

| | A | B |
|---|---|---|
| 1 | Product Name | |
| 2 | " Apple " | =TRIM(A2) |
| 3 | "Banana " | |
| 4 | " Cherry Pie " | |

**Step 3:** Press `Enter`. Cell B2 will display "Apple", with the extra spaces removed.

| | A | B |
|---|---|---|
| 1 | Product Name | |
| 2 | " Apple " | " Apple " |
| 3 | "Banana " | |
| 4 | " Cherry Pie " | |

**Step 4:** Drag the formula from B2 down to B4 to fill the remaining cells. Cells B3 and B4 will display "Banana" and "Cherry Pie", respectively, with all unnecessary spaces removed.

| ◢ | A | B |
|---|---|---|
| 1 | Product Name | |
| 2 | " Apple " | " Apple " |
| 3 | "Banana " | "Banana " |
| 4 | " Cherry Pie " | " Cherry Pie " |
| 5 | | |

---

**Advanced Tips:**

**1. Combining with Other Functions:** You can combine `TRIM` with other text functions like `UPPER`, `LOWER`, or `PROPER` to further format and clean your text data.

**2. Non-breaking Spaces:** The `TRIM` function doesn't remove non-breaking spaces (often entered with `Alt + 0160`). If you suspect these are in your data, you might need additional steps to remove them.

**3. Regular Use:** If you frequently import or copy data from external sources, consider using `TRIM` as a regular step in your data preparation process.

---

# Function #66 - SUM

The SUM function in Excel is one of the most fundamental and frequently used functions. It allows users to quickly total up a series of numbers without having to do manual calculations. Whether you're managing a budget, analyzing sales data, or just trying to figure out how much you spent on coffee last month, the SUM function is your go-to tool.

**Benefits:**

**1. Efficiency:** No need to manually add numbers – the SUM function does it instantly.

**2. Flexibility:** Works across rows, columns, or a combination of both.

**3. Dynamic:** If the data changes, the sum automatically updates.

**4. Versatility:** Can be combined with other functions for more advanced calculations.

---

**Step-by-Step Guide:**

**1. Basic Summation:**

- Click on the cell where you want the sum to appear.
- Type

| `=SUM(`. |
|---|

- Now, select the range of cells you want to sum up. For instance, if you want to sum cells A1 through A10, click and drag from A1 to A10.
- Close the parenthesis `)`.
- Press Enter.

### 2. Using the AutoSum Feature:
- Highlight the cells you want to sum.
- Click on the "AutoSum" button (it looks like an uppercase sigma: Σ) in the toolbar. Excel will automatically insert the SUM function.

### 3. Summing Non-Adjacent Cells:
- In the cell where you want the sum to appear, type `=SUM(`.
- Click on the first cell you want to include, then hold down the Ctrl key (Cmd on Mac) and click on any other cells you want to include.
- Close the parenthesis `)` and press Enter.

---

### Example:

### Downloadable example:
https://tinyurl.com/102-excel-functions

Imagine you have a list of monthly sales figures:

| | | A | | |
|---|---|---|---|---|

| ------- | --------- |
| 1 | January |
| 2 | 5000 |
| 3 | February |
| 4 | 5500 |
| 5 | March |
| 6 | 5200 |

|  | A |
|---|---|
| 1 | January |
| 2 | 5000 |
| 3 | February |
| 4 | 5500 |
| 5 | March |
| 6 | 5200 |

To find the total sales for the first quarter:

1. Click on cell A7.
2. Type `=SUM(`.
3. Drag to select cells A2 through A6.
4. Close the parenthesis `)` and press Enter.

|  | A |
|---|---|
| 1 | January |
| 2 | 5000 |
| 3 | February |
| 4 | 5500 |
| 5 | March |
| 6 | 5200 |
| 7 | =SUM(A1:A6) |

Cell A7 will now display the value 15700, which is the total sales for January, February, and March combined.

| | A |
|---|---|
| 1 | January |
| 2 | 5000 |
| 3 | February |
| 4 | 5500 |
| 5 | March |
| 6 | 5200 |
| 7 | 15700 |

---

**Advanced Tip:**

The SUM function can also be used in combination with other functions. For instance, `=SUM(A2:A10)/COUNT(A2:A10)` would give you the average of the numbers in cells A2 through A10. The possibilities are vast, making the SUM function not just a basic tool, but also a building block for more complex calculations.

---

# Function #67 - MINUTE

The `MINUTE` function in Excel is used to extract the minute component from a given time value. It returns a number between 0 (inclusive) and 59 (inclusive), representing the minute segment of the time.

Primary benefits of the `MINUTE` function include:

**1. Time Analysis:** Helps in breaking down and analyzing time data by isolating the minute component.

**2. Data Transformation:** Useful in converting time data into a format that can be more easily analyzed or presented.

**3. Enhanced Calculations:** Assists in performing calculations that specifically target the minute component of time values.

---

## Step-by-Step Guide

**Step 1:** Open your Excel workbook and navigate to the worksheet where you want to use the `MINUTE` function.

**Step 2:** Click on the cell where you want the extracted minute value to appear.

**Step 3:** Enter the `MINUTE` function. The syntax for the function is:

---

**=MINUTE(serial_number)**

---

- `serial_number` is the Excel time from which you want to extract the minute.

**Step 4:** After entering the desired time or cell reference containing the time, press `Enter`.

---

### Example

**Downloadable example:**
https://tinyurl.com/102-excel-functions

Imagine you have a dataset of event timestamps, and you want to extract the minute component from each timestamp.

Data:

A1: Timestamp      B1: Minute
A2: 9:15:30 AM     B2: ?
A3: 3:45:20 PM     B3: ?

A4: 12:05:55 PM      B4: ?

| | A | B |
|---|---|---|
| 1 | Timestamp | Minute |
| 2 | 9:15:30 AM | |
| 3 | 3:45:20 PM | |
| 4 | 12:05:55 PM | |

**Step 1:** Click on cell B2.

**Step 2:** Enter the formula to extract the minute component from the timestamp in A2:

=MINUTE(A2)

| | A | B |
|---|---|---|
| 1 | Timestamp | Minute |
| 2 | 9:15:30 AM | =MINUTE(A2) |
| 3 | 3:45:20 PM | |
| 4 | 12:05:55 PM | |
| 5 | | |

**Step 3:** Press `Enter`. Cell B2 will display "15", which is the minute component of the timestamp in A2.

**Step 4:** Drag the formula from B2 down to B4 to fill the remaining cells. Cells B3 and B4 will display "45" and "5", respectively.

| | A | B |
|---|---|---|
| 1 | Timestamp | Minute |
| 2 | 9:15:30 AM | 15 |
| 3 | 3:45:20 PM | 45 |
| 4 | 12:05:55 PM | 5 |
| 5 | | |

**Advanced Tips:**

**1. Combining with Other Functions:** You can combine `MINUTE` with other time functions like `HOUR` or `SECOND` to extract different components of a timestamp.

**2. Formatting:** Ensure that the cells you're extracting minutes from are correctly formatted as time values. If not, the `MINUTE` function might not work as expected.

**3. Use in Calculations:** The extracted minute values can be used in further calculations, such as determining average minutes or summing up total minutes.

# Function #68 - CONVERT

The `CONVERT` function in Excel is used to convert a number from one measurement system to another. It can handle a wide variety of unit conversions, from length and weight to temperature, time, and more.

Primary benefits of the `CONVERT` function include:

**1. Versatility:** It supports a broad range of unit conversions, eliminating the need for manual conversion tables or external tools.
**2. Accuracy:** Ensures precise conversions, reducing the risk of errors that can occur with manual calculations.
**3. Efficiency:** Streamlines data analysis and reporting when dealing with diverse units of measure.

---

## Step-by-Step Guide

**Step 1:** Open your Excel workbook and navigate to the worksheet where you want to use the `CONVERT` function.

**Step 2:** Click on the cell where you want the converted value to appear.

**Step 3:** Enter the `CONVERT` function. The syntax for the function is:

---

**=CONVERT(number, from_unit, to_unit)**

---

- `number` is the value you want to convert.
- `from_unit` is the unit of the number.
- `to_unit` is the unit you want to convert to.

> ➤ **Depending on your country, the ' , ' must be replaced by ' ; '**

**Step 4:** After entering the desired values and units, press `Enter`.

---

## Example

**Downloadable example:**
https://tinyurl.com/102-excel-functions

Imagine you have a dataset of distances in miles, and you want to convert them to kilometers.

Data:

A1: Distance (miles)   B1: Distance (km)
A2: 10          B2: ?
A3: 50          B3: ?
A4: 100          B4: ?

| | A | B |
|---|---|---|
| 1 | Distance (miles) | Distance (km) |
| 2 | 10 | |
| 3 | 50 | |
| 4 | 100 | |

**Step 1:** Click on cell B2.

**Step 2:** Enter the formula to convert the distance in A2 from miles to kilometers:

=CONVERT(A2, "mi", "km")

| | A | B | C |
|---|---|---|---|
| 1 | Distance (miles) | Distance (km) | |
| 2 | 10 | =CONVERT(A2; "mi"; "km") | |
| 3 | 50 | | |
| 4 | 100 | | |
| 5 | | | |

**Step 3:** Press `Enter`. Cell B2 will display the distance in kilometers, which is approximately "16.0934" km for 10 miles.

**Step 4:** Drag the formula from B2 down to B4 to fill the remaining cells. Cells B3 and B4 will display the converted distances for 50 and 100 miles, respectively.

| | A | B |
|---|---|---|
| 1 | Distance (miles) | Distance (km) |
| 2 | 10 | 16,09344 |
| 3 | 50 | 80,4672 |
| 4 | 100 | 160,9344 |

---

**Advanced Tips:**

**1. Supported Units**: Excel provides a wide range of units that the `CONVERT` function can handle. To see a full list, you can refer to Excel's official documentation or use the function's tooltip.

**2. Combining with Other Functions**: You can combine `CONVERT` with other functions to perform more complex calculations based on the converted values.

**3. Rounding:** If you want to present the converted values in a more readable format, consider using functions like `ROUND` to round the results to a specified number of decimal places.

# Function #69 - COUNTIFS

The `COUNTIFS` function in Excel counts the number of cells within a range that meet multiple conditions. It's an extension of the `COUNTIF` function, which handles only one condition.

Primary benefits of the `COUNTIFS` function include:

**1. Multiple Criteria:** Allows for counting based on multiple conditions, providing more flexibility than `COUNTIF`.

**2. Data Analysis:** Essential for analyzing large datasets to derive insights based on specific criteria.

**3. Dynamic Reporting:** Enables the creation of dynamic reports where counts can be updated as criteria change.

---

## Step-by-Step Guide

**Step 1:** Open your Excel workbook and navigate to the worksheet where you want to use the `COUNTIFS` function.

**Step 2:** Click on the cell where you want the count to appear.

**Step 3:** Enter the `COUNTIFS` function. The syntax for the function is:

---
**=COUNTIFS(range1, criteria1, [range2, criteria2], ...)**

---

- `range1` is the first range of cells you want to count.
- `criteria1` is the condition for the first range.
- Additional ranges and criteria can be added as needed.

> ➢ **Depending on your country, the ' , ' must be replaced by ' ; '**

**Step 4:** After entering the desired ranges and criteria, press `Enter`.

---

## Example

### Downloadable example:
https://tinyurl.com/102-excel-functions

Imagine you have a dataset of sales data, and you want to count the number of sales made by a specific salesperson for a particular product.

Data:

A1: Salesperson    B1: Product    C1: Quantity
A2: John         B2: Laptop    C2: 5
A3: Jane         B3: Phone     C3: 3
A4: John         B4: Laptop    C4: 7
A5: Jane         B5: Laptop    C5: 2
A6: John         B6: Phone     C6: 4

|   | A | B | C |
|---|---|---|---|
| 1 | Salesperson | Product | Quantity |
| 2 | John | Laptop | 5 |
| 3 | Jane | Phone | 3 |
| 4 | John | Laptop | 7 |
| 5 | Jane | Laptop | 2 |
| 6 | John | Phone | 4 |
| 7 |  |  |  |

Goal: Count the number of sales made by "John" for the product "Laptop".

**Step 1:** Click on an empty cell, say D2.

**Step 2:** Enter the formula to count the sales made by John for Laptops:

=COUNTIFS(A2:A6, "John", B2:B6, "Laptop")

| | A | B | C | D | E | F |
|---|---|---|---|---|---|---|
| 1 | Salesperson | Product | Quantity | =COUNTIFS(A2:A6;"John"; B2:B6; "Laptop") | | |
| 2 | John | Laptop | 5 | | | |
| 3 | Jane | Phone | 3 | | | |
| 4 | John | Laptop | 7 | | | |
| 5 | Jane | Laptop | 2 | | | |
| 6 | John | Phone | 4 | | | |
| 7 | | | | | | |

**Step 3:** Press `Enter`. Cell D2 will display "2", which is the number of sales John made for Laptops.

| | A | B | C | D |
|---|---|---|---|---|
| 1 | Salesperson | Product | Quantity | 2 |
| 2 | John | Laptop | 5 | |
| 3 | Jane | Phone | 3 | |
| 4 | John | Laptop | 7 | |
| 5 | Jane | Laptop | 2 | |
| 6 | John | Phone | 4 | |

---

**Advanced Tips:**

**1. Using Wildcards:** You can use wildcards like `*` and `?` in your criteria. For example, `"J*"` would count all salespersons whose names start with "J".

**2. Combining with Other Functions:** `COUNTIFS` can be combined with other functions for more complex analyses, such as `SUMIFS` for conditional summing.

**3. Handling Dates:** When working with dates, ensure your criteria are correctly formatted to match the date format in your data.

# Function #70 - COUNT

The `COUNT` function in Excel is used to count the number of cells within a range that contain numbers. It's particularly useful when you want to quickly determine how many cells in a given range have numerical data.

Primary benefits of the `COUNT` function include:

**1. Data Integrity:** Helps in identifying how many cells in a dataset have numerical values, which can be useful for data cleaning and validation.

**2. Simple Analysis:** Provides a quick way to understand the density of numerical data in large datasets.

**3. Versatility:** Can be combined with other functions for more complex analyses.

---

## Step-by-Step Guide

**Step 1:** Open your Excel workbook and navigate to the worksheet where you want to use the `COUNT` function.

**Step 2:** Click on the cell where you want the count to appear.

**Step 3:** Enter the `COUNT` function. The syntax for the function is:

---

**=COUNT(value1, [value2], ...)**

- `value1, value2, ...` are the values or ranges you want to count.

> ➢ **Depending on your country, the ' , ' must be replaced by ' ; '**

**Step 4:** After entering the desired values or ranges, press `Enter`.

---

**Example**

**Downloadable example:**
https://tinyurl.com/102-excel-functions

Imagine you have a dataset of scores for a class test, and you want to determine how many students have received scores (i.e., how many cells have numerical values).

Data:

A1: Student Name    B1: Score
A2: John        B2: 85
A3: Jane        B3:
A4: Alice       B4: 90
A5: Bob         B5:
A6: Charlie       B6: 78

| | A | B |
|---|---|---|
| 1 | Student Name | Score |
| 2 | John | 85 |
| 3 | Jane | |
| 4 | Alice | 90 |
| 5 | Bob | |
| 6 | Charlie | 78 |
| 7 | | |

Goal: Count the number of students who have received scores.

**Step 1:** Click on an empty cell, say C2.

**Step 2:** Enter the formula to count the scores:

=COUNT(B2:B6)

| | A | B | C |
|---|---|---|---|
| 1 | Student Name | Score | |
| 2 | John | 85 | =COUNT(B2:B6) |
| 3 | Jane | | |
| 4 | Alice | 90 | |
| 5 | Bob | | |
| 6 | Charlie | 78 | |

Step 3: Press `Enter`. Cell C2 will display "3", which is the number of students who have received scores.

| | A | B | C |
|---|---|---|---|
| 1 | Student Name | Score | |
| 2 | John | 85 | 3 |
| 3 | Jane | | |
| 4 | Alice | 90 | |
| 5 | Bob | | |
| 6 | Charlie | 78 | |
| 7 | | | |

---

**Advanced Tips:**

**1. Distinguishing from COUNTA:** While `COUNT` counts cells with numbers, `COUNTA` counts non-empty cells, regardless of content. Ensure you're using the right function for your needs.

2. Handling Errors: `COUNT` does not count cells with error values. If you want to count those, consider using functions like `COUNTA` or other specialized functions.

3. Combining Ranges: You can count across multiple ranges by separating them with commas, e.g., `=COUNT(B2:B6, D2:D6)`.

---

# Function #71 - IF

The `IF` function in Excel is a logical function that returns one value if a condition is true and another value if it's false. It's essentially a way to make simple decisions within your spreadsheet.

Primary benefits of the `IF` function include:

**1. Decision Making:** Enables logical operations within your spreadsheet, allowing for dynamic content based on conditions.
**2. Data Analysis:** Helps in categorizing or flagging data based on certain criteria.
**3. Enhanced Reporting:** Allows for the creation of more insightful and interactive reports.

---

**Step-by-Step Guide**

**Step 1:** Open your Excel workbook and navigate to the worksheet where you want to use the `IF` function.

**Step 2:** Click on the cell where you want the result to appear.

**Step 3:** Enter the `IF` function. The syntax for the function is:

---

=IF(logical_test, value_if_true, value_if_false)

---

- `logical_test` is the condition you want to check.
- `value_if_true` is the value that will be returned if the condition is true.
- `value_if_false` is the value that will be returned if the condition is false.

> ➤ **Depending on your country, the ' , ' must be replaced by ' ; '**

**Step 4:** After entering the desired condition and return values, press `Enter`.

---

### Example

**Downloadable example:**
https://tinyurl.com/102-excel-functions

Imagine you have a dataset of student scores, and you want to determine if each student has passed or failed based on a passing score of 50.

Data:

A1: Student Name    B1: Score    C1: Status
A2: John          B2: 45      C2: ?
A3: Jane          B3: 55      C3: ?
A4: Alice        B4: 49      C4: ?

| | A | B | C |
|---|---|---|---|
| 1 | Student Name | Score | Status |
| 2 | John | 45 | |
| 3 | Jane | 55 | |
| 4 | Alice | 49 | |

**Goal:** Determine the status (Passed/Failed) of each student.

**Step 1:** Click on cell C2.

**Step 2:** Enter the formula to determine John's status:

=IF(B2>=50, "Passed", "Failed")

| | A | B | C | D |
|---|---|---|---|---|
| 1 | Student Name | Score | Status | |
| 2 | John | 45 | =IF(B2>=50; "Passed"; "Failed") | |
| 3 | Jane | 55 | | |
| 4 | Alice | 49 | | |
| 5 | | | | |

**Step 3:** Press `Enter`. Cell C2 will display "Failed" since John's score is below 50.

**Step 4:** Drag the formula from C2 down to C4 to fill the remaining cells. Cells C3 and C4 will display the statuses for Jane and Alice, respectively.

| | A | B | C |
|---|---|---|---|
| 1 | Student Name | Score | Status |
| 2 | John | 45 | Failed |
| 3 | Jane | 55 | Passed |
| 4 | Alice | 49 | Failed |
| 5 | | | |

---

**Advanced Tips:**

**1. Nested IFs:** You can nest multiple `IF` functions to handle more than two outcomes. For example, grading (A, B, C, D, F) based on score ranges.

**2. Combining with Other Functions:** The `IF` function can be combined with other functions for more complex logic, such as `AND` and `OR` for multi-condition checks.

**3. Handling Errors:** To manage potential errors in your logic, consider combining `IF` with functions like `ISERROR` or `IFERROR`.

# Function #72 - AVERAGEIF

The `AVERAGEIF` function in Excel calculates the average of numbers in a range that meet a single condition or criterion. It's an extension of the basic `AVERAGE` function, but with the added capability of considering only those values that meet a specified condition.

Primary benefits of the `AVERAGEIF` function include:

**1. Selective Analysis:** Enables you to focus on specific subsets of your data.
**2. Data Insights:** Helps in deriving insights from data by considering only relevant data points.
**3. Efficiency:** Eliminates the need for manual filtering or additional calculations.

---

**Step-by-Step Guide**

**Step 1:** Open your Excel workbook and navigate to the worksheet where you want to use the `AVERAGEIF` function.

**Step 2:** Click on the cell where you want the average to appear.

**Step 3:** Enter the `AVERAGEIF` function. The syntax for the function is:

---
**=AVERAGEIF(range, criteria, [average_range])**
---

- `range` is the range of cells you want to average.
- `criteria` is the condition that defines which cells will be averaged.
- `[average_range]` (optional) is the actual set of cells to average. If omitted, `range` is used.

> ➤ **Depending on your country, the ' , ' must be replaced by ' ; '**

**Step 4:** After entering the desired range, criteria, and average range (if different from the criteria range), press `Enter`.

---

**Example**

**Downloadable example:**
https://tinyurl.com/102-excel-functions

Imagine you have a dataset of student scores for a test, and you want to determine the average score of students who scored above 50.

Data:

A1: Student Name    B1: Score
A2: John        B2: 45
A3: Jane        B3: 55
A4: Alice       B4: 49
A5: Bob        B5: 60

| | A | B |
|---|---|---|
| 1 | Student Name | Score |
| 2 | John | 45 |
| 3 | Jane | 55 |
| 4 | Alice | 49 |
| 5 | Bob | 60 |
| 6 | | |

Goal: Calculate the average score of students who scored more than 50.

**Step 1:** Click on an empty cell, say C2.

**Step 2:** Enter the formula to compute the average for scores above 50:

=AVERAGEIF(B2:B5, ">50")

| | A | B | C | D |
|---|---|---|---|---|
| 1 | Student Name | Score | | |
| 2 | John | 45 | =AVERAGEIF(B2:B5; ">50") | |
| 3 | Jane | 55 | | |
| 4 | Alice | 49 | | |
| 5 | Bob | 60 | | |
| 6 | | | | |

**Step 3:** Press `Enter`. Cell C2 will display "57.5", which is the average score of Jane and Bob, the two students who scored above 50.

| | A | B | C |
|---|---|---|---|
| 1 | Student Name | Score | |
| 2 | John | 45 | 57,5 |
| 3 | Jane | 55 | |
| 4 | Alice | 49 | |
| 5 | Bob | 60 | |
| 6 | | | |

**Advanced Tips:**

**1. Using Cells for Criteria:** Instead of hardcoding values like ">50", you can use a reference to another cell that contains the criterion.

**2. Handling Text:** `AVERAGEIF` can also handle text criteria, e.g., averaging values corresponding to a specific category or label.

**3. Multiple Conditions:** If you need to average based on multiple conditions, consider using the `AVERAGEIFS` function.

# Function #73 - UPPER

The `UPPER` function in Excel is a text function that converts all letters in a given text string to uppercase. It's particularly useful when standardizing text data or preparing data for systems that require uppercase inputs.

Primary benefits of the `UPPER` function include:

**1. Data Standardization:** Ensures consistency in datasets by converting all text to uppercase.

**2. Data Preparation:** Useful when preparing data for systems or databases that require or prefer uppercase inputs.

**3. Enhanced Readability:** In certain contexts, uppercase text can be more visually striking or easier to read.

---

## Step-by-Step Guide

**Step 1:** Open your Excel workbook and navigate to the worksheet where you want to use the `UPPER` function.

**Step 2:** Click on the cell where you want the uppercase text to appear.

**Step 3:** Enter the `UPPER` function. The syntax for the function is:

| =UPPER(text) |
| --- |

- `text` is the text string or cell reference you want to convert to uppercase.

**Step 4:** After entering the desired text or cell reference, press `Enter`.

---

### Example

**Downloadable example:**
https://tinyurl.com/102-excel-functions

Imagine you have a dataset of product names, and you want to standardize them by converting them all to uppercase.

Data:

A1: Product Name
A2: apple
A3: Banana
A4: Cherry Pie

| | A |
|---|---|
| 1 | Product Name |
| 2 | apple |
| 3 | Banana |
| 4 | Cherry Pie |
| 5 | |

Goal: Convert the product names to uppercase.

**Step 1:** Click on an empty cell adjacent to the data, say B2.

| | A | B |
|---|---|---|
| 1 | Product Name | |
| 2 | apple | =UPPER(A2) |
| 3 | Banana | |
| 4 | Cherry Pie | |

**Step 2:** Enter the formula to convert the product name "apple" to uppercase:

=UPPER(A2)

**Step 3:** Press `Enter`. Cell B2 will display "APPLE".

| | A | B |
|---|---|---|
| 1 | Product Name | |
| 2 | apple | APPLE |
| 3 | Banana | |
| 4 | Cherry Pie | |
| 5 | | |

**Step 4:** Drag the formula from B2 down to B4 to fill the remaining cells. Cells B3 and B4 will display "BANANA" and "CHERRY PIE", respectively.

| ◢ | A | B |
|---|---|---|
| 1 | Product Name | |
| 2 | apple | APPLE |
| 3 | Banana | BANANA |
| 4 | Cherry Pie | CHERRY PIE |

---

**Advanced Tips:**

**1. Combining with Other Functions**: The `UPPER` function can be combined with other text functions for more complex text manipulations. For instance, using `TRIM` before `UPPER` can remove any leading or trailing spaces before converting to uppercase.

**2. Case Sensitivity:** Remember that the `UPPER` function will convert all characters to uppercase. If you need to maintain the original case for certain parts of the text, you'll need to use a different approach or function.

---

# Function #74 - OR

The `OR` function in Excel is a logical function used to test multiple conditions and returns `TRUE` if any of the conditions are true, and `FALSE` if all conditions are false. It's especially useful when you need to evaluate multiple criteria and determine if any one of them holds true.

Primary benefits of the `OR` function include:

**1. Flexibility:** Allows for the evaluation of multiple conditions simultaneously.

**2. Decision Making:** Helps in making decisions based on a variety of criteria.

**3. Combination with Other Functions:** Can be combined with other functions like `IF` to create more complex logical tests.

---

**Step-by-Step Guide**

**Step 1:** Open your Excel workbook and navigate to the worksheet where you want to use the `OR` function.

**Step 2:** Click on the cell where you want the result (TRUE or FALSE) to appear.

**Step 3:** Enter the `OR` function. The syntax for the function is:

---

**=OR(logical1, [logical2], ...)**

---

- `logical1, logical2, ...` are the conditions you want to test.

> ➢ **Depending on your country, the ' , ' must be replaced by ' ; '**

**Step 4:** After entering the desired conditions, press `Enter`.

---

## Example

**Downloadable example:**
https://tinyurl.com/102-excel-functions

Imagine you have a dataset of students and their scores in two subjects. You want to identify if any student has scored above 90 in either of the subjects.

Data:

A1: Student Name    B1: Math Score    C1: Science Score

A2: John        B2: 85        C2: 92

A3: Jane        B3: 91        C3: 88

A4: Alice       B4: 89        C4: 90

| | A | B | C |
|---|---|---|---|
| 1 | Student Name | Math Score | Science Score |
| 2 | John | 85 | 92 |
| 3 | Jane | 91 | 88 |
| 4 | Alice | 89 | 90 |
| 5 | | | |

Goal: Determine if a student has scored above 90 in either Math or Science.

**Step 1:** Click on an empty cell adjacent to the data, say D2.

Step 2: Enter the formula to check if John has scored above 90 in either subject:

=OR(B2>90, C2>90)

| | A | B | C | D | E |
|---|---|---|---|---|---|
| 1 | Student Name | Math Score | Science Score | | |
| 2 | John | 85 | 92 | =OR(B2>90; C2>90) | |
| 3 | Jane | 91 | 88 | | |
| 4 | Alice | 89 | 90 | | |

Step 3: Press `Enter`. Cell D2 will display `TRUE` since John has scored 92 in Science.

315

| | A | B | C | D |
|---|---|---|---|---|
| 1 | Student Name | Math Score | Science Score | |
| 2 | John | 85 | 92 | TRUE |
| 3 | Jane | 91 | 88 | |
| 4 | Alice | 89 | 90 | |
| 5 | | | | |

Step 4: Drag the formula from D2 down to D4 to fill the remaining cells. Cells D3 will display `TRUE` (since Jane scored 91 in Math), and D4 will display `FALSE`.

| | A | B | C | D |
|---|---|---|---|---|
| 1 | Student Name | Math Score | Science Score | |
| 2 | John | 85 | 92 | TRUE |
| 3 | Jane | 91 | 88 | TRUE |
| 4 | Alice | 89 | 90 | FALSE |

---

**Advanced Tips:**

**1. Combining with IF:** The `OR` function can be combined with the `IF` function to perform actions based on the result. For example: `=IF(OR(B2>90, C2>90), "High Scorer", "Average Scorer")`.

**2. Multiple Conditions:** The `OR` function can evaluate up to 255 conditions, giving you a lot of flexibility in your logical tests.

---

# Function #75 - RANDBETWEEN

The `RANDBETWEEN` function in Excel is used to generate a random integer between two specified numbers, inclusive. This function can be particularly useful in scenarios like simulations, random sampling, and even in games.

Primary benefits of the `RANDBETWEEN` function include:

**1. Random Sampling:** Useful for selecting a random sample from a dataset.
**2. Simulations:** Can be employed in financial modeling and other simulations where random numbers are required.
**3. Data Generation:** Handy for generating mock data for testing or demonstration purposes.

---

## Step-by-Step Guide

**Step 1:** Open your Excel workbook and navigate to the worksheet where you want to use the `RANDBETWEEN` function.

**Step 2:** Click on the cell where you want the random number to appear.

**Step 3:** Enter the `RANDBETWEEN` function. The syntax for the function is:

---
**=RANDBETWEEN(bottom, top)**
---

- `bottom` is the smallest integer in the range.
- `top` is the largest integer in the range.

> ➢ **Depending on your country, the ' , ' must be replaced by ' ; '**

**Step 4:** After entering the desired range, press `Enter`.

---

## Example

**Downloadable example:**
https://tinyurl.com/102-excel-functions

Imagine you're organizing a raffle draw, and you have ticket numbers ranging from 1001 to 2000. You want to randomly select a winning ticket number.

**Step 1:** Click on an empty cell, say A1.

**Step 2:** Enter the formula to generate a random ticket number between 1001 and 2000:

=RANDBETWEEN(1001, 2000)

| | A | B |
|---|---|---|
| 1 | =RANDBETWEEN(1001; 2000) | |
| 2 | | |
| 3 | | |

**Step 3:** Press `Enter`. Cell A1 will display a random number between 1001 and 2000.

| | A | B |
|---|---|---|
| 1 | 1970 | |
| 2 | | |
| 3 | | |
| 4 | | |

**Note:** Every time the worksheet recalculates, the `RANDBETWEEN` function will generate a new random number. To prevent this, you can copy the cell with the random number and then use "Paste Special" to paste it as a value.

**Advanced Tips:**

**1. Generating Random Decimals:** If you need random decimal numbers, you can use a combination of `RAND` and `RANDBETWEEN`. For example, to get a random decimal between 1 and 2, you could use: `=1 + RAND()`.

**2. Static Random Numbers:** As mentioned, `RANDBETWEEN` recalculates with every worksheet change. To keep the generated number static, copy the cell and paste it as a value.

# Function #76 - MOD

The `MOD` function in Excel returns the remainder after a number is divided by a divisor. In mathematical terms, it provides the modulus of the division. This function can be particularly useful in scenarios like determining the parity of numbers, creating cyclical patterns, and more.

Primary benefits of the `MOD` function include:

**1. Cyclical Patterns:** Useful for creating repeating patterns in data.
**2. Parity Checks:** Helps in determining if a number is even or odd.
**3. Financial Calculations:** Assists in evenly distributing amounts in budgeting or scheduling scenarios.

---

## Step-by-Step Guide

**Step 1:** Open your Excel workbook and navigate to the worksheet where you want to use the `MOD` function.

**Step 2:** Click on the cell where you want the result to appear.

**Step 3:** Enter the `MOD` function. The syntax for the function is:

| =MOD(number, divisor) |
|---|

- `number` is the number for which you want to find the remainder.
- `divisor` is the number by which division is to be performed.

> ➤ **Depending on your country, the ' , ' must be replaced by ' ; '**

**Step 4:** After entering the desired numbers, press `Enter`.

---

## Example

**Downloadable example:**
https://tinyurl.com/102-excel-functions

Imagine you're scheduling employees for a 7-day work week, and you want to determine which day an employee will be off based on their employee number.

Data:

A1: Employee Number    B1: Day Off
A2: 1
A3: 2
A4: 3
... and so on

| | A | B |
|---|---|---|
| 1 | Employee Number | Day Off |
| 2 | 1 | |
| 3 | 2 | |
| 4 | 3 | |

Goal: Determine the day off for each employee based on their employee number.

**Step 1:** Click on cell B2.

**Step 2:** Enter the formula to determine the day off for the employee with number 1:

=MOD(A2, 7)

| | A | B |
|---|---|---|
| 1 | Employee Number | Day Off |
| 2 | 1 | =MOD(A2; 7) |
| 3 | 2 | |
| 4 | 3 | |

**Step 3:** Press `Enter`. Cell B2 will display a number between 0 and 6 (both inclusive).

| | A | B |
|---|---|---|
| 1 | Employee Number | Day Off |
| 2 | 1 | 1 |
| 3 | 2 | |
| 4 | 3 | |

**Step 4:** Drag the formula from B2 down to fill the remaining cells. This will give the day off for each employee.

**Note:** You can further use a lookup table or nested `IF` statements to convert the numbers 0-6 to actual day names (e.g., Sunday, Monday, etc.).

---

**Advanced Tips:**

**1. Checking Even or Odd:** The `MOD` function can be used to check if a number is even or odd. For example, `=MOD(A2, 2)` will return 0 for even numbers and 1 for odd numbers.

**2. Cyclical Patterns:** If you want to create a pattern that repeats every 'n' rows, the `MOD` function can be combined with the `ROW` function.

---

# Function #77 - COLUMNS

The `COLUMNS` function in Excel returns the number of columns in a specified array or reference. It's particularly useful when you're working with dynamic ranges, array formulas, or when setting up data validation lists that can expand or contract based on user input.

Primary benefits of the `COLUMNS` function include:

**1. Dynamic Ranges:** Helps in creating formulas that can adapt to changing data ranges.
**2. Array Formulas:** Assists in determining the size of arrays when working with array formulas.
**3. Data Validation:** Useful in setting up dynamic drop-down lists.

---

## Step-by-Step Guide

**Step 1:** Open your Excel workbook and navigate to the worksheet where you want to use the `COLUMNS` function.

**Step 2:** Click on the cell where you want the result to appear.

**Step 3:** Enter the `COLUMNS` function. The syntax for the function is:

| =COLUMNS(array) |
|---|

- `array` is the range of cells for which you want to determine the number of columns.

**Step 4:** After entering the desired range, press `Enter`.

---

**Example**

**Downloadable example:**
https://tinyurl.com/102-excel-functions

Imagine you have a dataset of monthly sales figures, and you want to determine how many months of data you have.

Data:

A1: January    B1: February    C1: March

| | A | B | C |
|---|---|---|---|
| 1 | January | February | March |
| 2 | | | |

Goal: Determine the number of months (columns) with data.

**Step 1:** Click on an empty cell, say A3.

**Step 2:** Enter the formula to determine the number of months:

=COLUMNS(A1:C1)

| | A | B | C |
|---|---|---|---|
| 1 | January | February | March |
| 2 | | | |
| 3 | =COLUMNS(A1:C1) | | |
| 4 | | | |

**Step 3:** Press `Enter`. Cell A3 will display the number 3, indicating there are 3 months (columns) in the range.

| | A | B | C |
|---|---|---|---|
| 1 | January | February | March |
| 2 | | | |
| 3 | 3 | | |
| 4 | | | |

**Advanced Tips:**

**1. Dynamic Column Counting:** If you're unsure about the end column of your data, you can combine the `COLUMNS` function with other functions like `INDEX` to dynamically count columns.

**2. Data Validation:** When creating a dynamic drop-down list, you can use the `COLUMNS` function to determine the range of the list based on the number of columns with data.

# Function #78 - TIME

The `TIME` function in Excel returns a decimal number between 0 (zero) and 1, representing a particular time of day, based on given hours, minutes, and seconds. This function is especially useful when you need to create, manipulate, or calculate time values.

Primary benefits of the `TIME` function include:

**1. Data Creation:** Easily create time values for data entry or simulation.

**2. Time Calculations:** Combine with other time values for arithmetic operations.

**3. Data Transformation:** Convert raw time data (like hours, minutes, and seconds) into a unified time format.

---

## Step-by-Step Guide

**Step 1:** Open your Excel workbook and navigate to the worksheet where you want to use the `TIME` function.

**Step 2:** Click on the cell where you want the time value to appear.

**Step 3:** Enter the `TIME` function. The syntax for the function is:

---

| **=TIME(hour, minute, second)** |
| :---: |

---

- `hour` is the hour component of the time.
- `minute` is the minute component.
- `second` is the second component.

> ➢ **Depending on your country, the ' , ' must be replaced by ' ; '**

**Step 4:** After entering the desired values, press `Enter`.

---

## Example

**Downloadable example:**
https://tinyurl.com/102-excel-functions

Imagine you're setting up a daily schedule, and you want to represent the start time of a particular event.

Data:

A1: Event Name     B1: Start Time

## A2: Morning Jog

| | A | B |
|---|---|---|
| 1 | Event Name | Start Time |
| 2 | Morning Jog | |
| 3 | | |
| 4 | | |

Goal: Set the start time for the "Morning Jog" event at 6:30:00 AM.

**Step 1:** Click on cell B2.

**Step 2:** Enter the formula to represent the start time:

=TIME(6, 30, 0)

| | A | B |
|---|---|---|
| 1 | Event Name | Start Time |
| 2 | Morning Jog | =TIME(6;30; 0) |
| 3 | | |

**Step 3:** Press `Enter`. Cell B2 will display the time as 6:30 AM (the display format might vary based on your regional settings and Excel's default time format).

| | A | B |
|---|---|---|
| 1 | Event Name | Start Time |
| 2 | Morning Jog | 6:30 AM |
| 3 | | |

**Advanced Tips:**

**1. Time Arithmetic:** You can add or subtract the results of the `TIME` function to perform time-based arithmetic. For instance, if you want to calculate the end time of the jog, assuming it lasts 45 minutes, you could use `B2 + TIME(0,45,0)`.

**2. Combining with Date:** The `TIME` function can be combined with the `DATE` function to create a full date-time value. For example, `=DATE(2023,5,15) + TIME(6,30,0)` would represent 6:30 AM on May 15, 2023.

# Function #79 - ROUND

The `ROUND` function in Excel is used to round a number to a specified number of digits. This function is essential when you need to present data in a more readable format, especially in financial, scientific, or statistical contexts.

Primary benefits of the `ROUND` function include:

**1. Data Presentation:** Makes numerical data more readable by rounding to a specific number of decimal places.

**2. Accuracy:** Ensures calculations are based on standardized values, especially when dealing with financial data.

**3. Data Consistency:** Helps in maintaining uniformity in datasets by rounding numbers to a consistent level of precision.

---

**Step-by-Step Guide**

**Step 1:** Open your Excel workbook and navigate to the worksheet where you want to use the `ROUND` function.

**Step 2:** Click on the cell where you want the rounded number to appear.

**Step 3:** Enter the `ROUND` function. The syntax for the function is:

| =ROUND(number, num_digits) |
| --- |

- `number` is the value you want to round.
- `num_digits` specifies the number of digits to which you want to round the number.

> ➢ **Depending on your country, the ' , ' must be replaced by ' ; '**

**Step 4:** After entering the desired values, press `Enter`.

---

**Example**

**Downloadable example:**
https://tinyurl.com/102-excel-functions

Imagine you're calculating the average monthly sales for a product, and the result is $1234.56789. You want to present this value rounded to two decimal places for clarity.

Data:

A1: Average Monthly Sales
A2: $1234.56789

| | A | B |
|---|---|---|
| 1 | Average Monthly Sales | |
| 2 | 1234,56789 | |
| 3 | | |

Goal: Round the average monthly sales value to two decimal places.

**Step 1:** Click on an empty cell, say A3.

**Step 2:** Enter the formula to round the value in A2 to two decimal places:

=ROUND(A2, 2)

| | A | B |
|---|---|---|
| 1 | Average Monthly Sales | |
| 2 | 1234,56789 | |
| 3 | =ROUND(A2; 2) | |
| 4 | | |

**Step 3:** Press `Enter`. Cell A3 will display the value as $1234.57.

| | A | B | C |
|---|---|---|---|
| 1 | Average Monthly Sales | | |
| 2 | 1234,56789 | | |
| 3 | 1234,57 | | |
| 4 | | | |
| 5 | | | |

**Advanced Tips:**

**1. Rounding to Whole Numbers:** If you want to round to the nearest whole number, set `num_digits` to 0. For example, `=ROUND(123.456, 0)` will give 123.

**2. Rounding to Tens, Hundreds, etc.:** You can use negative values for `num_digits` to round to the nearest ten, hundred, etc. For instance, `=ROUND(123.456, -1)` will give 120.

# Function #80 - CLEAN

The `CLEAN` function in Excel is used to remove non-printable characters from a text string. These characters can often be found in data imported from other applications or systems and can cause issues with data processing or display.

Primary benefits of the `CLEAN` function include:

**1. Data Integrity:** Ensures that your text data is free from hidden or non-printable characters that might disrupt further processing or analysis.

**2. Improved Readability:** Helps in presenting data without unexpected symbols or characters.

**3. Data Compatibility:** Makes sure that your data is compatible across different systems or applications by removing potential problematic characters.

---

## Step-by-Step Guide

**Step 1:** Open your Excel workbook and navigate to the worksheet where you want to use the `CLEAN` function.

**Step 2:** Click on the cell where you want the cleaned data to appear.

**Step 3:** Enter the `CLEAN` function. The syntax for the function is:

---

## =CLEAN(text)

---

- `text` is the string from which you want to remove non-printable characters.

**Step 4:** After entering the desired value or cell reference, press `Enter`.

---

## Example

**Downloadable example:**
https://tinyurl.com/102-excel-functions

Scenario: Imagine you've imported a list of product names from an external system, and some of the names have non-printable characters causing display issues.

Data:

A1: Product Name
A2: ProductA [non-printable character]
A3: ProductB [non-printable character]

| | A | B | C |
|---|---|---|---|
| 1 | Product Name | | |
| 2 | ProductA [non-printable character] | | |
| 3 | ProductB [non-printable character] | | |
| 4 | | | |
| 5 | | | |
| 6 | | | |

Goal: Clean the product names from non-printable characters.

**Step 1:** Click on an empty cell, say B2.

**Step 2:** Enter the formula to clean the value in A2:

=CLEAN(A2)

**Step 3:** Press `Enter`. Cell B2 will display the cleaned product name as "ProductA".

**Step 4:** Drag the formula down to clean other product names in the list.

**Advanced Tips:**

**1. Combining with TRIM:** Often, in addition to non-printable characters, data might have extra spaces. You can combine `CLEAN` with the `TRIM` function to remove both non-printable characters and extra spaces. For example, `=TRIM(CLEAN(A2))`.

**2. Identifying Non-Printable Characters:** If you're curious about which non-printable characters are in your data, you can use the `CODE` function to identify the ASCII value of the first character in a text string.

# Function #81 - OFFSET

The `OFFSET` function in Excel returns a cell or range reference that is a specified number of rows and columns from a given starting point. It's particularly useful when you need to create dynamic ranges or retrieve values based on variable criteria.

Primary benefits of the `OFFSET` function include:

**1. Dynamic Data Retrieval:** Easily fetch data based on changing conditions or criteria.

**2. Flexibility:** Create dynamic named ranges that can expand or contract based on data.

**3. Advanced Data Analysis:** Use in conjunction with other functions for more complex data manipulations.

---

## Step-by-Step Guide

**Step 1:** Open your Excel workbook and navigate to the worksheet where you want to use the `OFFSET` function.

**Step 2:** Click on the cell where you want the result to appear.

**Step 3:** Enter the `OFFSET` function. The syntax for the function is:

> **=OFFSET(reference, rows, cols, [height], [width])**

- `reference`: The starting point.
- `rows`: The number of rows to move from the starting point (can be positive, negative, or zero).
- `cols`: The number of columns to move from the starting point (can be positive, negative, or zero).
- `[height]` (optional): The height of the returned reference.
- `[width]` (optional): The width of the returned reference.

> ➤ **Depending on your country, the ' , ' must be replaced by ' ; '**

**Step 4:** After entering the desired parameters, press `Enter`.

---

## Example

**Downloadable example:**
https://tinyurl.com/102-excel-functions

Imagine you have a table of monthly sales data, and you want to retrieve the sales value for a particular month based on an input.

Data:

A1: January   B1: $5000
A2: February  B2: $5500
A3: March     B3: $5200

| | A | B | C |
|---|---|---|---|
| 1 | January | 5000 | |
| 2 | February | 5500 | |
| 3 | March | 5200 | |
| 4 | | | |

Goal: Retrieve the sales value for the month specified in cell D1.

**Step 1:** In cell D1, enter the month number (e.g., 1 for January, 2 for February).

| | A | B | C | D |
|---|---|---|---|---|
| 1 | January | 5000 | | 1 |
| 2 | February | 5500 | | |
| 3 | March | 5200 | | |

**Step 2:** In cell E1, enter the formula to fetch the sales value based on the month number in D1:

=OFFSET(B1, D1-1, 0)

| ▲ | A | B | C | D | E | F |
|---|---|---|---|---|---|---|
| 1 | January | 5000 | | 2 | =OFFSET(B1; D1-1; 0) | |
| 2 | February | 5500 | | | | |
| 3 | March | 5200 | | | | |
| 4 | | | | | | |

**Step 3:** Press `Enter`. If you entered "2" in D1, cell E1 will display the value "$5500" corresponding to February.

| ▲ | A | B | C | D | E | F |
|---|---|---|---|---|---|---|
| 1 | January | 5000 | | 2 | 5500 | |
| 2 | February | 5500 | | | | |
| 3 | March | 5200 | | | | |

---

**Advanced Tips:**

**1. Dynamic Ranges:** `OFFSET` can be used to create dynamic named ranges. For instance, if you have a list that grows over time, you can use `OFFSET` combined with `COUNTA` to create a range that expands automatically.

**2. Combining with Other Functions:** `OFFSET` can be combined with functions like `SUM`, `AVERAGE`, etc., to perform calculations on dynamic ranges.

**3. Avoid Excessive Use:** While `OFFSET` is powerful, excessive use can slow down Excel, especially in large spreadsheets. Use it judiciously.

---

# Function #82 - YEAR

The `YEAR` function in Excel is used to extract the year from a given date. It returns the year as a four-digit number, making it particularly useful when you need to categorize, filter, or analyze data based on years.

Primary benefits of the `YEAR` function include:

**1. Data Segmentation:** Easily categorize or group data by year.

**2. Simplified Analysis**: Analyze trends or patterns over the years.

**3. Date Manipulation:** Use in conjunction with other date functions for more complex date calculations.

---

## Step-by-Step Guide

**Step 1:** Open your Excel workbook and navigate to the worksheet where you want to use the `YEAR` function.

**Step 2:** Click on the cell where you want the result to appear.

**Step 3:** Enter the `YEAR` function. The syntax for the function is:

| =YEAR(serial_number) |
| --- |

- `serial_number`: The date from which you want to extract the year.

**Step 4:** After entering the desired date or cell reference containing the date, press `Enter`.

---

**Example**

**Downloadable example:**
https://tinyurl.com/102-excel-functions

Imagine you have a list of birthdates, and you want to determine the birth year for each individual.

Data:

A1: Name      B1: Birthdate
A2: Alice     B2: 15/03/1990
A3: Bob       B3: 22/07/1985
A4: Charlie   B4: 05/10/2000

| ◢ | A | B | C |
|---|---|---|---|
| 1 | Name | Birthdate | |
| 2 | Alice | 15/03/1990 | |
| 3 | Bob | 22/07/1985 | |
| 4 | Charlie | 05/10/2000 | |
| 5 | | | |
| 6 | | | |

Goal: Extract the birth year for each individual.

**Step 1:** Click on an empty cell next to the first birthdate, say C2.

**Step 2:** Enter the formula to extract the year from the birthdate in B2:

=YEAR(B2)

| ◢ | A | B | C |
|---|---|---|---|
| 1 | Name | Birthdate | |
| 2 | Alice | 15/03/1990 | =YEAR(B2) |
| 3 | Bob | 22/07/1985 | |
| 4 | Charlie | 05/10/2000 | |
| 5 | | | |

**Step 3:** Press `Enter`. Cell C2 will display the value "1990".

| ◢ | A | B | C | D |
|---|---|---|---|---|
| 1 | Name | Birthdate | | |
| 2 | Alice | 15/03/1990 | 1990 | |
| 3 | Bob | 22/07/1985 | | |
| 4 | Charlie | 05/10/2000 | | |
| 5 | | | | |

**Step 4:** Drag the formula down to extract the birth years for the other individuals in the list.

| ▲ | A | B | C |
|---|---|---|---|
| 1 | Name | Birthdate | |
| 2 | Alice | 15/03/1990 | 1990 |
| 3 | Bob | 22/07/1985 | 1985 |
| 4 | Charlie | 05/10/2000 | 2000 |

**Advanced Tips:**

**1. Combining with Other Functions:** The `YEAR` function can be combined with other date functions like `MONTH` or `DAY` to extract different parts of a date.

**2. Age Calculation:** You can use the `YEAR` function along with the `TODAY` function to calculate the age of an individual. For example, `=YEAR(TODAY()) - YEAR(B2)` would give the age of Alice based on her birthdate in B2.

# Function #83 - LEN

The `LEN` function in Excel is used to determine the number of characters in a text string. This includes letters, numbers, special characters, and even spaces.

Primary Benefits of the LEN Function:

**1. Data Validation:** Ensure that data entries, like phone numbers or identification codes, meet a specific length requirement.

**2. Text Manipulation:** Assist in other text functions by providing the length of a string, which can be crucial for functions like `LEFT`, `RIGHT`, or `MID`.

**3. Data Analysis:** Analyze textual data to find out average lengths, outliers, or other patterns based on text length.

---

## Step-by-Step Guide

**Step 1:** Open your Excel workbook and navigate to the worksheet where you want to use the `LEN` function.

**Step 2:** Click on the cell where you want the result to appear.

**Step 3:** Enter the `LEN` function. The syntax for the function is:

=LEN(text)

- `text`: The text string for which you want to determine the length.

**Step 4:** After entering the desired text or cell reference containing the text, press `Enter`.

---

## Example

**Downloadable example:**
https://tinyurl.com/102-excel-functions

Imagine you have a list of product codes, and you want to determine the length of each code.

Data:

A1: Product Name   B1: Product Code
A2: Widget A       B2: WDG-A123
A3: Gadget B       B3: GDT-B4567
A4: Tool C         B4: TL-C89

| | A | B | C |
|---|---|---|---|
| 1 | Product Name | Product Code | |
| 2 | Widget A | WDG-A123 | |
| 3 | Gadget B | GDT-B4567 | |
| 4 | Tool C | TL-C89 | |
| 5 | | | |

Goal: Determine the length of each product code.

**Step 1:** Click on an empty cell next to the first product code, say C2.

**Step 2:** Enter the formula to determine the length of the product code in B2:

=LEN(B2)

| | A | B | C |
|---|---|---|---|
| 1 | Product Name | Product Code | |
| 2 | Widget A | WDG-A123 | =LEN(B2) |
| 3 | Gadget B | GDT-B4567 | |
| 4 | Tool C | TL-C89 | |
| 5 | | | |

**Step 3:** Press `Enter`. Cell C2 will display the value "8", which is the length of "WDG-A123".

| | A | B | C |
|---|---|---|---|
| 1 | Product Name | Product Code | |
| 2 | Widget A | WDG-A123 | 8 |
| 3 | Gadget B | GDT-B4567 | |
| 4 | Tool C | TL-C89 | |
| 5 | | | |

Step 4: Drag the formula down to determine the lengths for the other product codes in the list.

| ▲ | A | B | C |
|---|---|---|---|
| 1 | Product Name | Product Code | |
| 2 | Widget A | WDG-A123 | 8 |
| 3 | Gadget B | GDT-B4567 | 9 |
| 4 | Tool C | TL-C89 | 6 |

# Advanced Tips:

**1. Combining with Other Functions:** The `LEN` function can be combined with other functions for more advanced text manipulations. For instance, to determine the number of actual characters without spaces, you can use `=LEN(B2) - LEN(SUBSTITUTE(B2, " ", ""))`.

**2. Data Cleaning:** The `LEN` function can be instrumental when cleaning up data, especially when trying to find cells with unexpected lengths which might indicate erroneous data.

# Function #84 - ROWS

The `ROWS` function in Excel returns the number of rows in a reference or array. It's particularly useful when you want to determine the size of a particular range in terms of its row count.

Primary Benefits of the ROWS Function:

**1. Dynamic Range Size:** Easily determine the size of a range, especially when combined with other functions.

**2. Data Validation:** Ensure that data sets or tables have the expected number of rows.

**3. Automation:** Use in conjunction with other functions for creating dynamic formulas that adjust based on the number of rows in a dataset.

---

## Step-by-Step Guide

**Step 1:** Open your Excel workbook and navigate to the worksheet where you want to use the `ROWS` function.

**Step 2:** Click on the cell where you want the result to appear.

**Step 3:** Enter the `ROWS` function. The syntax for the function is:

| =ROWS(array) |
|---|

- `array`: The range or array from which you want to determine the number of rows.

**Step 4:** After entering the desired range or array, press `Enter`.

---

**Example**

**Downloadable example:**
https://tinyurl.com/102-excel-functions

Imagine you have a list of employees, and you want to determine the number of employees listed.

Data:

A1: Employee Name
A2: John Doe
A3: Jane Smith
A4: Robert Brown

| ◢ | A | B |
|---|---|---|
| 1 | Employee Name | |
| 2 | John Doe | |
| 3 | Jane Smith | |
| 4 | Robert Brown | |
| 5 | | |

Goal: Determine the number of employees in the list.

**Step 1:** Click on an empty cell, say B1.

**Step 2:** Enter the formula to determine the number of rows (employees) in column A starting from A2:

=ROWS(A2:A1048576)           -
COUNTBLANK(A2:A1048576)

| ◢ | A | B | C | D | E | F |
|---|---|---|---|---|---|---|
| 1 | Employee Name | =ROWS(A2:A1048576) - COUNTBLANK(A2:A1048576) | | | | |
| 2 | John Doe | | | | | |
| 3 | Jane Smith | | | | | |
| 4 | Robert Brown | | | | | |
| 5 | | | | | | |

This formula counts all the rows from A2 to the end of the column, then subtracts any blank cells to give the actual number of employees.

**Step 3:** Press `Enter`. Cell B1 will display the value "3", which is the number of employees listed.

| | A | B |
|---|---|---|
| 1 | Employee Name | 3 |
| 2 | John Doe | |
| 3 | Jane Smith | |
| 4 | Robert Brown | |
| 5 | | |

**Advanced Tips:**

**1. Dynamic Ranges:** The `ROWS` function can be combined with other functions like `OFFSET` to create dynamic ranges that adjust based on the number of rows in a dataset.

**2. Array Formulas:** In more advanced scenarios, `ROWS` can be used within array formulas to process and return results for multiple rows of data simultaneously.

# Function #85 - IFERROR

The `IFERROR` function in Excel is used to trap and handle errors in a formula. If the formula results in an error, `IFERROR` will return a specified value, otherwise, it will return the formula's result.

Primary Benefits of the IFERROR Function:

**1. Error Management:** Easily handle errors in formulas without displaying confusing error messages to users.

**2. Cleaner Spreadsheets:** Prevent unsightly error values (like `#DIV/0!`, `#VALUE!`, etc.) from appearing in your worksheets.

**3. Custom Messages:** Provide custom error messages or values, making your spreadsheets more user-friendly.

**4. Efficiency:** Simplify complex formulas by handling potential errors directly within the formula.

---

## Step-by-Step Guide

**Step 1:** Open your Excel workbook and navigate to the worksheet where you want to use the `IFERROR` function.

**Step 2:** Click on the cell where you want the result to appear.

**Step 3:** Enter the `IFERROR` function. The syntax for the function is:

| =IFERROR(value, value_if_error) |
| --- |

- `value`: The expression or formula you want to evaluate.
- `value_if_error`: The value or action to take if the `value` results in an error.

➤ **Depending on your country, the ' , ' must be replaced by ' ; '**

**Step 4:** After entering the desired formula and error handling value, press `Enter`.

---

**Example**

**Downloadable example:**
https://tinyurl.com/102-excel-functions

Imagine you have a list of sales and costs, and you want to calculate the profit margin. However, in some cases, the cost might be zero, leading to a division error.

Data:

A1: Sales    B1: Costs
A2: 100      B2: 50
A3: 150      B3: 0
A4: 200      B4: 100

Goal: Calculate the profit margin without displaying error messages.

| | A | B |
|---|---|---|
| 1 | Sales | Costs |
| 2 | 100 | 50 |
| 3 | 150 | 0 |
| 4 | 200 | 100 |

**Step 1:** Click on C1 and label it "Profit Margin".

**Step 2:** In cell C2, enter the formula to calculate the profit margin, but use `IFERROR` to handle potential division errors:

=IFERROR(A2/B2, "N/A")

| | A | B | C | D | E |
|---|---|---|---|---|---|
| 1 | Sales | Costs | | | |
| 2 | 100 | 50 | =IFERROR(A2/B2; "N/A") | | |
| 3 | 150 | 0 | | | |
| 4 | 200 | 100 | | | |

**Step 3:** Drag the formula down to apply it to the other cells in column C.

The result in C3 will display "N/A" because B3 has a value of 0, leading to a division error. Instead of displaying an error message, `IFERROR` provides a cleaner "N/A" result.

| ⊿ | A | B | C | D |
|---|---|---|---|---|
| 1 | Sales | Costs | | |
| 2 | 100 | 50 | 2 | |
| 3 | 150 | 0 | N/A | |
| 4 | 200 | 100 | 2 | |
| 5 | | | | |

**Advanced Tips:**

**1. Combining with Other Functions:** `IFERROR` can be combined with other Excel functions to create more complex error-handling formulas.
**2. Nested Error Handling:** You can nest multiple `IFERROR` functions to handle different types of errors with different responses.

# Function #86 - MODE

The `MODE` function in Excel is used to find the most frequently occurring number in a set of numbers. In statistical terms, this number is called the mode.

Primary Benefits of the MODE Function:

**1. Statistical Analysis:** Quickly identify the most common value in a dataset.
**2. Data Insights:** Understand trends or preferences in data by identifying which values appear most often.
**3. Simplicity:** Easily determine the mode without having to sort or manually count individual numbers.
4. Versatility: Useful in various fields, from business analytics to academic research.

---

## Step-by-Step Guide

**Step 1:** Open your Excel workbook and navigate to the worksheet containing your data.

**Step 2:** Click on the cell where you want the mode to appear.

**Step 3:** Enter the `MODE` function. The syntax for the function is:

| =MODE(number1, [number2], ...) |
|---|

- `number1, number2, ...`: The numbers for which you want to find the mode.

➢ **Depending on your country, the ' , ' must be replaced by ' ; '**

**Step 4:** After entering the desired range or numbers, press `Enter`.

---

### Example

**Downloadable example:**
https://tinyurl.com/102-excel-functions

Imagine you have a list of student grades, and you want to determine the most frequently awarded grade.

Data:

A1: Grades
A2: 85
A3: 90

A4: 85

A5: 92

A6: 87

A7: 90

A8: 85

| | A |
|---|---|
| 4 | 85 |
| 5 | 92 |
| 6 | 87 |
| 7 | 90 |
| 8 | 85 |
| 9 | |

Goal: Identify the most common grade.

**Step 1:** Click on B1 and label it "Mode Grade".

**Step 2:** In cell B2, enter the formula to calculate the mode:

=MODE(A2:A8)

| | A | B |
|---|---|---|
| 1 | Grades | |
| 2 | 85 | =MODE(A2:A8) |
| 3 | 90 | |
| 4 | 85 | |
| 5 | 92 | |
| 6 | 87 | |
| 7 | 90 | |
| 8 | 85 | |
| 9 | | |

**Step 3:** Press `Enter`.

The result in B2 will display "85" because it is the most frequently occurring grade in the list.

| ⁄ | A | B |
|---|---|---|
| 1 | Grades | |
| 2 | 85 | 85 |
| 3 | 90 | |
| 4 | 85 | |
| 5 | 92 | |
| 6 | 87 | |
| 7 | 90 | |
| 8 | 85 | |

---

**Advanced Tips:**

**1. Handling No Mode:** If there's no repeating number, the `MODE` function will return a `#N/A` error. You can use the `IFERROR` function to handle this and display a custom message.

**2. MODE.MULT:** In Excel, there's also a `MODE.MULT` function that returns an array of modes if a dataset has multiple modes.

**3. Non-Numeric Data:** Remember, `MODE` is designed for numeric data. For non-numeric data, you might need to use other methods or tools to determine the mode.

# Function #87 - SUBTOTAL

The `SUBTOTAL` function in Excel provides a way to perform various mathematical operations, such as counting, summing, or averaging, on a range of cells. One of its unique features is that it automatically ignores rows that are hidden by a filter or manually, making it especially useful in tables or ranges with applied filters.

Primary Benefits of the SUBTOTAL Function:

**1. Versatility:** It can perform multiple functions, from summing to counting to finding the maximum or minimum value.

**2. Dynamic Calculation:** Automatically excludes hidden rows in its calculations.

**3. Simplicity:** Reduces the need for complex formulas when working with filtered data.

**4. Integration with Filters:** Works seamlessly with Excel's filtering tools, ensuring accurate calculations even when data views change.

---

## Step-by-Step Guide

**Step 1:** Open your Excel workbook and navigate to the worksheet containing your data.

**Step 2:** Click on the cell where you want the subtotal result to appear.

**Step 3:** Enter the `SUBTOTAL` function. The syntax for the function is:

=SUBTOTAL(function_num, ref1, [ref2], ...)

- `function_num`: A number representing the function you want to use (e.g., 9 for SUM, 1 for AVERAGE).
- `ref1, ref2, ...`: The range of cells on which you want to perform the operation.

> ➢ **Depending on your country, the ' , ' must be replaced by ' ; '**

**Step 4:** After entering the desired function number and range, press `Enter`.

---

**Example**

**Downloadable example:**
https://tinyurl.com/102-excel-functions

Imagine you have a list of sales data for a month, and you've applied a filter to view only a specific product's sales. You want to find the sum of the filtered sales.

Data:

A1: Product
B1: Sales
A2: Apples
B2: $100
A3: Bananas
B3: $150
A4: Apples
B4: $120
A5: Grapes
B5: $80

| | A | B |
|---|---|---|
| 1 | Product | Sales |
| 2 | Apples | 100 |
| 3 | Bananas | 150 |
| 4 | Apples | 120 |
| 5 | Grapes | 80 |

Goal: Sum the sales of the filtered product.

**Step 1:** Apply a filter to column A to view only "Apples".

**Step 2:** Click on B6 (or an empty cell) to display the total sales for the filtered product.

**Step 3:** Enter the formula to calculate the subtotal:

=SUBTOTAL(9, B2:B5)

Here, "9" represents the SUM function.

| | A | B | C | D |
|---|---|---|---|---|
| 1 | Product | Sales | | |
| 2 | Apples | 100 | | |
| 3 | Bananas | 150 | | |
| 4 | Apples | 120 | | |
| 5 | Grapes | 80 | | |
| 6 | | =SUBTOTAL(9; B2:B5) | | |
| 7 | | | | |

**Step 4:** Press `Enter`.

If you change the filter to another product, the subtotal will automatically update to reflect the sum of the visible rows.

---

**Advanced Tips:**

**1. Function Numbers:** The `SUBTOTAL` function has two sets of function numbers: 1-11 and 101-111. The first set (1-11) includes all rows, while the second set (101-111) excludes rows hidden manually but includes those hidden by filters.

**2. Nested SUBTOTALs:** If you have nested `SUBTOTAL` functions, the inner `SUBTOTAL` functions are ignored to prevent double counting.

# Function #88 - SECOND

The `SECOND` function in Excel is designed to extract the seconds component from a given time value. It's a useful function when you're working with detailed time data and need to separate or analyze the seconds specifically.

Primary Benefits of the SECOND Function:

**1. Precision:** Allows for detailed time analysis by focusing on the seconds component.
2. Simplicity: Provides a straightforward way to extract seconds without complex formulas.
3. Data Transformation: Useful for converting time data into a more digestible format for reports or further calculations.

---

## Step-by-Step Guide

**Step 1:** Open your Excel workbook and navigate to the worksheet containing your time data.

**Step 2:** Click on the cell where you want the extracted seconds to appear.

**Step 3:** Enter the `SECOND` function. The syntax for the function is:

| =SECOND(serial_number) |
| --- |

- `serial_number`: This is the Excel time from which you want to extract the seconds.

**Step 4:** After entering the time value or cell reference containing the time, press `Enter`.

---

## Example

**Downloadable example:**
https://tinyurl.com/102-excel-functions

Imagine you have a list of exact times at which certain events occurred, and you want to analyze the seconds component of each event time.

Data:

A1: Event Time
A2: 10:15:45
A3: 14:32:20
A4: 18:45:55

| | A |
|---|---|
| 1 | Event Time |
| 2 | 10:15:45 |
| 3 | 14:32:20 |
| 4 | 18:45:55 |

Goal: Extract the seconds from each event time.

**Step 1:** Click on B2 (or an adjacent empty cell) to display the seconds for the first event time.

**Step 2:** Enter the formula to extract the seconds:

=SECOND(A2)

| | A | B |
|---|---|---|
| 1 | Event Time | |
| 2 | 10:15:45 | =SECOND(A2) |
| 3 | 14:32:20 | |
| 4 | 18:45:55 | |

**Step 3:** Press `Enter`.

The result in B2 will display "45", which represents the seconds from the time in A2.

**Step 4:** Drag the formula down to extract seconds for the other event times.

| | A | B |
|---|---|---|
| 1 | Event Time | |
| 2 | 10:15:45 | 45 |
| 3 | 14:32:20 | 20 |
| 4 | 18:45:55 | 55 |

**Advanced Tips:**

**1. Time Formatting:** Ensure that the cells containing your time data are formatted as 'Time' in Excel. This ensures that the `SECOND` function can correctly interpret the values.

**2. Combining with Other Functions:** The `SECOND` function can be combined with other time functions like `HOUR` and `MINUTE` to extract and analyze different components of a time value.

# Function #89 - WEEKDAY

The `WEEKDAY` function in Excel is designed to return the day of the week corresponding to a date. The day is given as an integer, ranging from 1 (Sunday) to 7 (Saturday), by default.

Primary Benefits of the WEEKDAY Function:

1. Analysis of Data by Day: It allows users to categorize or filter data based on the day of the week.
2. Flexibility: The function provides different numbering systems for days, catering to various needs.
3. Integration with Other Functions: Can be combined with other date and time functions for comprehensive date analyses.

---

## Step-by-Step Guide

**Step 1:** Open your Excel workbook and navigate to the worksheet containing your date data.

Step 2: Click on the cell where you want the day of the week to appear.

**Step 3:** Enter the `WEEKDAY` function. The syntax for the function is:

| =WEEKDAY(serial_number, [return_type]) |
| --- |

- `serial_number`: The date for which you want to find the day of the week.
- `[return_type]`: (Optional) A number that determines the return value. If omitted, it defaults to 1 (Sunday = 1, Saturday = 7).

> ➢ **Depending on your country, the ' , ' must be replaced by ' ; '**

**Step 4:** After entering the date value or cell reference containing the date, press `Enter`.

---

**Example**

**Downloadable example:**
https://tinyurl.com/102-excel-functions

Imagine you have a list of dates representing order placements, and you want to analyze on which day of the week most orders are placed.

Data:

A1: Order Date
A2: 2023-01-05
A3: 2023-02-05
A4: 2023-03-05

| | A | B |
|---|---|---|
| 1 | Order Date | |
| 2 | 01/05/2023 | |
| 3 | 02/05/2023 | |
| 4 | 03/05/2023 | |
| 5 | | |

Goal: Determine the day of the week for each order date.

**Step 1:** Click on B2 (or an adjacent empty cell) to display the day of the week for the first order date.

**Step 2:** Enter the formula to determine the day of the week:

=WEEKDAY(A2)

| | A | B |
|---|---|---|
| 1 | Order Date | |
| 2 | 01/05/2023 | =WEEKDAY(A2) |
| 3 | 02/05/2023 | 3 |
| 4 | 03/05/2023 | 4 |
| 5 | | |

**Step 3:** Press `Enter`.

The result in B2 will display "2", which represents Monday (if using the default return type).

**Step 4:** Drag the formula down to determine the day of the week for the other order dates.

| ▲ | A | B |
|---|---|---|
| 1 | Order Date | |
| 2 | 01/05/2023 | 2 |
| 3 | 02/05/2023 | 3 |
| 4 | 03/05/2023 | 4 |
| 5 | | |

---

**Advanced Tips:**

**1. Custom Return Types**: You can use different return types to adjust the starting day of the week. For instance, using a return type of 2 will make Monday = 1 and Sunday = 7.

**2. Day Name:** To get the actual name of the day, you can combine the `WEEKDAY` function with the `CHOOSE` function or use custom formatting.

---

# Function #90 - ISLOGICAL

The `ISLOGICAL` function in Excel is a straightforward yet powerful tool. It checks whether a value (or cell reference) is a logical value, i.e., `TRUE` or `FALSE`, and returns `TRUE` if it is, and `FALSE` otherwise.

Primary Benefits of the ISLOGICAL Function:

**1. Data Validation:** It can be used to ensure that certain cells contain only logical values.

**2. Error Prevention:** In complex formulas, ensuring that a particular value is logical can prevent errors.

**3. Enhanced Analysis:** When combined with other functions, it can be used to create more advanced logical tests.

---

## Step-by-Step Guide

**Step 1:** Open your Excel workbook and navigate to the worksheet where you want to use the function.

**Step 2:** Click on the cell where you want the result of the `ISLOGICAL` function to appear.

**Step 3:** Enter the `ISLOGICAL` function. The syntax for the function is simple:

| =ISLOGICAL(value) |
|---|

- `value`: The value or cell reference you want to test.

**Step 4:** After entering the desired value or cell reference, press `Enter`.

## Example

**Downloadable example:**
https://tinyurl.com/102-excel-functions

Imagine you have a list of values, and you want to check which of them are logical values.

Data:

A1: Value
A2: TRUE
A3: 100
A4: "Hello"
A5: FALSE

| | A |
|---|---|
| 1 | Value |
| 2 | TRUE |
| 3 | 100 |
| 4 | "Hello" |
| 5 | FALSE |

Goal: Determine which values in the list are logical.

**Step 1:** Click on B2 (or an adjacent empty cell) to display the result for the first value.

**Step 2:** Enter the formula to check if the value is logical:

| =ISLOGICAL(A2) |
|---|

| | A | B |
|---|---|---|
| 1 | Value | |
| 2 | TRUE | =ISLOGICAL(A2) |
| 3 | 100 | |
| 4 | "Hello" | |
| 5 | FALSE | |

**Step 3:** Press `Enter`.

The result in B2 will display "TRUE", indicating that the value in A2 is a logical value.

| | A | B |
|---|---|---|
| 1 | Value | |
| 2 | TRUE | TRUE |
| 3 | 100 | |
| 4 | "Hello" | |
| 5 | FALSE | |

**Step 4:** Drag the formula down to check the other values in the list.

The results will show "TRUE" for A2 and A5, and "FALSE" for A3 and A4.

| | A | B |
|---|---|---|
| 1 | Value | |
| 2 | TRUE | TRUE |
| 3 | 100 | FALSE |
| 4 | "Hello" | FALSE |
| 5 | FALSE | TRUE |
| 6 | | |

---

**Advanced Tips:**

**1. Combining with IF:** You can use `ISLOGICAL` within an `IF` statement to perform specific actions based on whether a value is logical. For example: `=IF(ISLOGICAL(A2), "Logical", "Not Logical")` would return "Logical" for A2 in our example.

**2. Data Cleaning:** If you're importing data from external sources, `ISLOGICAL` can help identify cells that contain unexpected logical values.

# Function #91 - AND

The `AND` function is a logical function in Excel that returns `TRUE` if all the conditions specified are true, and `FALSE` otherwise. It can test up to 255 conditions.

Primary Benefits of the AND Function:

**1. Multiple Condition Testing:** It allows you to test multiple conditions simultaneously.

**2. Enhanced Decision Making:** When combined with other functions, it can be used to make decisions based on multiple criteria.

**3. Data Validation:** It can be used to ensure that multiple conditions are met before proceeding with a calculation or action.

---

## Step-by-Step Guide

**Step 1:** Open your Excel workbook and navigate to the worksheet where you want to use the function.

**Step 2:** Click on the cell where you want the result of the `AND` function to appear.

**Step 3:** Enter the `AND` function. The syntax for the function is:

```
=AND(logical1, [logical2], ...)
```

- `logical1, logical2, ...`: The conditions you want to test.

> **Depending on your country, the ' , ' must be replaced by ' ; '**

**Step 4:** After entering the desired conditions, press `Enter`.

---

**Example**

**Downloadable example:**
https://tinyurl.com/102-excel-functions

Imagine you have a list of students with their scores in two subjects, and you want to identify which students scored above 50 in both subjects.

Data:

A1: Student Name   B1: Subject 1   C1: Subject 2
A2: John           B2: 55          C2: 60

A3: Jane       B3: 52       C3: 48
A4: Bob        B4: 60       C4: 65

| | A | B | C | D |
|---|---|---|---|---|
| 1 | Student Name | Subject 1 | Subject 2 | |
| 2 | John | 55 | 60 | |
| 3 | Jane | 52 | 48 | |
| 4 | Bob | 60 | 65 | |

Goal: Determine which students scored above 50 in both subjects.

**Step 1:** Click on D2 (or an adjacent empty cell) to display the result for the first student.

**Step 2:** Enter the formula to check if the student scored above 50 in both subjects:

=AND(B2>50, C2>50)

| | A | B | C | D | E |
|---|---|---|---|---|---|
| 1 | Student Name | Subject 1 | Subject 2 | | |
| 2 | John | 55 | | 60 | =AND(B2>50; C2>50) |
| 3 | Jane | 52 | | 48 | |
| 4 | Bob | 60 | | 65 | |

**Step 3:** Press `Enter`.

The result in D2 will display "TRUE", indicating that John scored above 50 in both subjects.

**Step 4:** Drag the formula down to check the scores for the other students.

The results will show "TRUE" for John and Bob, and "FALSE" for Jane.

| ⊿ | A | B | C | D |
|---|---|---|---|---|
| 1 | Student Name | Subject 1 | Subject 2 | |
| 2 | John | 55 | 60 | TRUE |
| 3 | Jane | 52 | 48 | FALSE |
| 4 | Bob | 60 | 65 | TRUE |
| 5 | | | | |

**Advanced Tips:**

**1. Combining with IF:** You can use `AND` within an `IF` statement to perform specific actions based on multiple conditions. For example: `=IF(AND(B2>50, C2>50), "Pass", "Fail")` would return "Pass" for John in our example.

**2. Nested AND:** You can nest multiple `AND` functions to test more complex conditions.

# Function #92 - NOW

The `NOW` function in Excel is a date and time function that returns the current date and time. The function does not have any arguments and will update the date and time every time the worksheet recalculates.

Primary Benefits of the NOW Function:

**1. Real-time Data:** It provides the current date and time, which can be useful for timestamping entries or calculations.

**2. Dynamic Updates:** The function updates automatically, ensuring you always have the most current date and time.

**3. Versatility:** It can be combined with other date and time functions for a wide range of applications.

---

## Step-by-Step Guide

**Step 1:** Open your Excel workbook and navigate to the worksheet where you want to use the function.

**Step 2:** Click on the cell where you want the current date and time to appear.

**Step 3:** Enter the `NOW` function. The syntax for the function is simple:

```
=NOW()
```

**Step 4:** Press `Enter`. The cell will now display the current date and time.

---

## Example

**Downloadable example:**
https://tinyurl.com/102-excel-functions

Imagine you're tracking tasks in a project, and you want to timestamp when each task is marked as completed.

Data:

A1: Task      B1: Status     C1: Completion Time
A2: Design       B2: Completed   C2:
A3: Development   B3: In Progress  C3:

Goal: Automatically timestamp the "Completion Time" when a task status is changed to "Completed".

| | A | B | C |
|---|---|---|---|
| 1 | Task | Status | Completion Time |
| 2 | Design | Completed | |
| 3 | Development | In Progress | |
| 4 | | | |

**Step 1:** Click on C2.

**Step 2:** Enter a formula that checks if the task is completed and, if so, timestamps it:

=IF(B2="Completed", NOW(), "")

| | A | B | C | D |
|---|---|---|---|---|
| 1 | Task | Status | Completion Time | |
| 2 | Design | Completed | =IF(B2="Completed";NOW();"") | |
| 3 | Development | In Progress | | |
| 4 | | | | |

**Step 3:** Press `Enter`.

If the task in A2 is marked as "Completed", C2 will display the current date and time. Otherwise, it will remain blank.

**Step 4:** Drag the formula down to apply it to other tasks.

| | A | B | C |
|---|---|---|---|
| 1 | Task | Status | Completion Time |
| 2 | Design | Completed | 24/08/2023 |
| 3 | Development | In Progress | |
| 4 | | | |

**Advanced Tips:**

**1. Formatting:** You can format the result of the `NOW` function to display only the date or time. Right-click the cell, select "Format Cells", and choose your preferred date or time format.

**2. Static Timestamp:** If you want a static timestamp that doesn't update, use `Ctrl + ,` for the date and `Ctrl + Shift + ,` for the time. This will enter the current date or time as a static value.

**3. Combining with Other Functions:** `NOW` can be combined with other functions for more complex operations, like calculating the difference between the current date and a due date.

# Function #93 - IFNA

The `IFNA` function is a specialized logical function in Excel that returns a value you specify if a formula results in the `#N/A` error, otherwise, it returns the result of the formula. This function is particularly useful when you want to handle `#N/A` errors gracefully without letting them disrupt your data presentation.

Primary Benefits of the IFNA Function:

**1. Error Handling:** It provides a clean way to handle `#N/A` errors that can arise from functions like `VLOOKUP` or `MATCH`.

**2. Data Presentation:** Ensures that your worksheets look professional and readable by replacing error messages with meaningful data or messages.

**3. Simplicity:** Offers a straightforward approach to handle one specific error, making it easier to use than the more general `IFERROR` function when you only care about `#N/A` errors.

---

## Step-by-Step Guide

**Step 1:** Open your Excel workbook and navigate to the worksheet where you want to use the function.

**Step 2:** Identify the formula or cell reference that might result in a `#N/A` error.

**Step 3:** Use the `IFNA` function to check for this error. The syntax for the function is:

---

**=IFNA(value, value_if_na)**

---

- `value`: This is the expression or cell reference you're checking.
- `value_if_na`: The value or message you want to display if `value` results in a `#N/A` error.

> ➢ **Depending on your country, the ' , ' must be replaced by ' ; '**

**Step 4:** Press `Enter` to apply the function.

---

## Example

**Downloadable example:**
https://tinyurl.com/102-excel-functions

You have a list of product IDs and you're using the `VLOOKUP` function to find their corresponding names from a master list. However, not all product IDs might have a match, leading to `#N/A` errors.

Data:

A1: Product ID    B1: Product Name
A2: 101           B2: =VLOOKUP(A2, MasterList, 2, FALSE)
A3: 102           B3: =VLOOKUP(A3, MasterList, 2, FALSE)

Goal: Replace any `#N/A` errors with the message "Not Found".

**Step 1:** Click on B2.

**Step 2:** Wrap the `VLOOKUP` function with `IFNA`:

=IFNA(VLOOKUP(A2, MasterList, 2, FALSE), "Not Found")

**Step 3:** Press `Enter`.

Now, if the product ID in A2 doesn't have a match in the master list, B2 will display "Not Found" instead of the `#N/A` error.

**Step 4:** Drag the formula down to apply it to other product IDs.

---

**Advanced Tips:**

**1. Combining with Other Functions:** While `IFNA` is designed for `#N/A` errors, if you want to handle all errors, you can use the `IFERROR` function.

**2. Nested Usage:** You can nest `IFNA` within other functions or even use it in conjunction with `IFERROR` to handle different errors in specific ways.

---

# Function #94 - RAND

The `RAND` function in Excel is a versatile tool that generates a random decimal number between 0 and 1. Each time a worksheet is recalculated or opened, the `RAND` function produces a new random number.

Primary Benefits of the RAND Function:

**1. Versatility:** Can be used in a variety of scenarios, from simulations to random sampling.
**2. No Arguments:** Unlike many other functions, `RAND` doesn't require any arguments, making it straightforward to use.
**3. Dynamic:** The function recalculates and produces a new random number whenever any change occurs in the worksheet.

---

### Step-by-Step Guide

**Step 1:** Open your Excel workbook and select the cell where you want to generate a random number.

**Step 2:** Enter the formula:

| =RAND() |
|---|

**Step 3:** Press `Enter`. The cell will now display a random decimal number between 0 and 1.

**Step 4:** If you want to generate a new random number, you can either:
- Make any change in the worksheet.
- Press `F9` to recalculate the worksheet.

---

**Example**

**Downloadable example:**
https://tinyurl.com/102-excel-functions

Scenario: Suppose you're a teacher and you want to randomly assign students to one of three groups. You have a list of student names and you want to use the `RAND` function to help with the assignment.

Data:

A1: Student Name    B1: Group
A2: Alice         B2:
A3: Bob           B3:

| | A | B |
|---|---|---|
| 1 | Student Name | Group |
| 2 | Alice | |
| 3 | Bob | |

Goal: Assign each student to Group 1, 2, or 3 based on a random number.

**Step 1:** Click on B2.

**Step 2:** Enter the formula:

=IF(RAND() < 0.33, "Group 1", IF(RAND() < 0.66, "Group 2", "Group 3"))

| | A | B | C | D | E | F |
|---|---|---|---|---|---|---|
| 1 | Student Name | Group | | | | |
| 2 | Alice | =IF(RAND() < 0,33; "Group 1"; IF(RAND() < 0,66; "Group 2"; "Group 3")) | | | | |
| 3 | Bob | Group 1 | | | | |
| 4 | | | | | | |

**Step 3:** Press `Enter`.

**Step 4:** Drag the formula down to apply it to the other student names.

Now, each student will be randomly assigned to one of the three groups.

| | A | B |
|---|---|---|
| 1 | Student Name | Group |
| 2 | Alice | Group 2 |
| 3 | Bob | Group 1 |

**Advanced Tips:**

**1. Generating Whole Numbers**: If you want to generate random whole numbers within a specific range, you can combine `RAND` with other functions. For example, to get a random number between 1 and 100: `=INT(RAND()*100) + 1`.

**2. Static Random Numbers:** If you want the random numbers to remain static (not change with every recalculation), after generating them with `RAND`, copy the cells and use "Paste Special" > "Values" to overwrite the formulas with their current values.

# Function #95 - NETWORKDAYS

The `NETWORKDAYS` function in Excel calculates the number of whole workdays between two specified dates (inclusive), excluding weekends and optionally specified holidays. This function is particularly useful in business scenarios where you need to compute the number of working days for tasks, projects, or other time-bound activities.

Primary Benefits of the NETWORKDAYS Function:

**1. Business Efficiency:** Easily calculate the number of working days between two dates, which aids in project planning and management.

**2. Flexibility:** Ability to exclude specific dates (like holidays) from the calculation.

**3. Standardization:** Provides a consistent method to compute working days, ensuring everyone is on the same page.

---

## Step-by-Step Guide

**Step 1:** Open your Excel workbook and select the cell where you want to display the number of working days.

**Step 2:** Enter the formula using the following syntax:

> **=NETWORKDAYS(start_date, end_date, [holidays])**

- `start_date`: The start date of the period.
- `end_date`: The end date of the period.
- `[holidays]`: (Optional) A range of dates that should be excluded from the working day calendar, such as public holidays.

> ➤ **Depending on your country, the ' , ' must be replaced by ' ; '**

**Step 3:** Press `Enter` to get the number of working days between the specified dates.

---

## Example

**Downloadable example:**
https://tinyurl.com/102-excel-functions

Imagine you're a project manager and you want to calculate the number of working days for a project that starts on January 1st and ends on January 31st. However, January 1st is a public holiday, and there's another holiday on January 15th.

Data:

A1: Start Date   B1: 01/01/2023
A2: End Date    B2: 01/31/2023
A3: Holidays    B3: 01/01/2023
          B4: 01/15/2023
A5: Working Days   B5: (This is where we'll use the formula)

| | A | B |
|---|---|---|
| 1 | Start Date | 01/01/2023 |
| 2 | End Date | 31/01/2023 |
| 3 | Holidays | 01/01/2023 |
| 4 | Working Days | 15/01/2023 |
| 5 | | |

**Step 1:** Click on B5.

**Step 2:** Enter the formula:

=NETWORKDAYS(B1, B2, B3:B4)

| | A | B | C |
|---|---|---|---|
| 1 | Start Date | 01/01/2023 | |
| 2 | End Date | 31/01/2023 | |
| 3 | Holidays | 01/01/2023 | |
| 4 | Working Days | 15/01/2023 | |
| 5 | | =NETWORKDAYS(B1; B2; B3:B4) | |

**Step 3:** Press `Enter`.

The result displayed in B5 will be `22`, indicating there are 22 working days in January 2023 when considering the two holidays.

| | A | B |
|---|---|---|
| 1 | Start Date | 01/01/2023 |
| 2 | End Date | 31/01/2023 |
| 3 | Holidays | 01/01/2023 |
| 4 | Working Days | 15/01/2023 |
| 5 | | 22 |

**Advanced Tips:**

**1. Using with Other Functions:** You can combine `NETWORKDAYS` with other functions for more complex calculations. For instance, if you want to calculate the end date of a project given a start date and a number of working days, you can use it with the `WORKDAY` function.

**2. Dynamic Holiday Lists:** Maintain a separate table or list for holidays, which you can update yearly or as needed. This way, you can reference this list dynamically in your `NETWORKDAYS` function.

# Function #96 - CODE

The `CODE` function in Excel returns a numeric code for the first character in a text string. The returned code corresponds to the character set used by your computer, which is typically the ASCII value for most standard characters.

Primary Benefits of the CODE Function:

**1. Data Analysis:** Helps in analyzing and understanding the underlying numeric codes of characters, especially when dealing with non-standard characters or symbols.

**2. Data Validation:** Useful in scenarios where specific characters need to be identified or filtered out.

**3. Interoperability:** Assists in data migration or transformation tasks where character encoding might be a concern.

---

## Step-by-Step Guide

**Step 1:** Open your Excel workbook and select the cell where you want to display the numeric code of a character.

**Step 2:** Enter the formula using the following syntax:

---

## =CODE(text)

---

- `text`: The text for which you want to return the code of the first character.

**Step 3:** Press `Enter` to get the numeric code of the specified character.

---

### Example

**Downloadable example:**
https://tinyurl.com/102-excel-functions

Imagine you're working with a dataset that contains special symbols, and you want to identify the ASCII value of these symbols to filter or replace them.

Data:

A1: Character     B1: !
A2: ASCII Code     B2: (This is where we'll use the formula)

| | A | B |
|---|---|---|
| 1 | Character | ! |
| 2 | ASCII Code | |

**Step 1:** Click on B2.

**Step 2:** Enter the formula:

=CODE(B1)

**Step 3:** Press `Enter`.

| | A | B |
|---|---|---|
| 1 | Character | ! |
| 2 | ASCII Code | =CODE(B1) |

The result displayed in B2 will be `33`, which is the ASCII value for the exclamation mark `!`.

| | A | B |
|---|---|---|
| 1 | Character | ! |
| 2 | ASCII Code | 33 |

## Advanced Tips:

**1. Using with Other Functions:** You can combine `CODE` with functions like `IF` or `VLOOKUP` to perform specific actions or lookups based on character codes.

**2. Understanding ASCII:** Familiarize yourself with the ASCII table to better understand the codes returned by the `CODE` function. This will help in scenarios where you need to identify specific ranges of characters.

**3. Decoding:** To reverse the process (i.e., to get a character from a code), you can use the `CHAR` function.

# Function #97 - SUMPRODUCT

The `SUMPRODUCT` function is a powerful and versatile function in Excel that multiplies corresponding components in the given arrays and returns the sum of those products. It's essentially a way to perform array multiplication followed by a summation.

Primary Benefits of the SUMPRODUCT Function:

**1. Array Calculations Without Array Formulas:** It allows you to perform array-style calculations without the need for entering them as array formulas.

**2. Weighted Averages:** Easily compute weighted averages without helper columns.

**3. Conditional Summing:** Sum data based on multiple conditions without using an array formula.

**4. Flexibility:** Can be combined with other functions for more complex calculations.

## Step-by-Step Guide

**Step 1:** Open your Excel workbook and select the cell where you want to display the result of the SUMPRODUCT function.

**Step 2:** Enter the formula using the following syntax:

> =SUMPRODUCT(array1, [array2], [array3], ...)

- `array1, array2, ...`: The arrays you want to multiply and then sum.

> ➤ **Depending on your country, the ' , ' must be replaced by ' ; '**

**Step 3:** Press `Enter` to get the result.

---

**Example**

**Downloadable example:**
https://tinyurl.com/102-excel-functions

Imagine you're a store manager and you want to calculate the total revenue from different products. You have the quantity sold in one column and the price per unit in another column.

Data:

A1: Product      B1: Quantity     C1: Price per unit
A2: Apples       B2: 10           C2: $2
A3: Bananas      B3: 5            C3: $1

A4: Cherries     B4: 8       C4: $3

| | A | B | C |
|---|---|---|---|
| 1 | Product | Quantity | Price per unit |
| 2 | Apples | 10 | 2 |
| 3 | Bananas | 5 | 1 |
| 4 | Cherries | 8 | 3 |
| 5 | | | |

**Step 1:** Click on a cell where you want the total revenue (let's say D1).

**Step 2:** Enter the formula:

=SUMPRODUCT(B2:B4, C2:C4)

| | A | B | C | D | E | F |
|---|---|---|---|---|---|---|
| 1 | Product | Quantity | Price per unit | =SUMPRODUCT(B2:B4; C2:C4) | | |
| 2 | Apples | 10 | 2 | | | |
| 3 | Bananas | 5 | 1 | | | |
| 4 | Cherries | 8 | 3 | | | |

**Step 3:** Press `Enter`.

The result displayed in D1 will be `$49`, which is the total revenue from the products.

| | A | B | C | D |
|---|---|---|---|---|
| 1 | Product | Quantity | Price per unit | 49 |
| 2 | Apples | 10 | 2 | |
| 3 | Bananas | 5 | 1 | |
| 4 | Cherries | 8 | 3 | |

**Advanced Tips:**

**1. Using with Conditions:** You can use the `--` (double unary) to convert Boolean values to numbers (TRUE to 1 and FALSE to 0) and use them in conditions. For example, to sum only the products that sold more than 6 units: `=SUMPRODUCT(--(B2:B4>6), B2:B4, C2:C4)`.

**2. Handling Non-Numeric Data:** Ensure that the arrays you're using with `SUMPRODUCT` do not contain non-numeric data, as this will result in an error.

**3. Combining with Other Functions:** `SUMPRODUCT` can be combined with functions like `LEN`, `VALUE`, and others to perform more complex calculations.

# Function #98 - DAY

The `DAY` function in Excel is a date and time function that returns the day of the month as a number from 1 to 31 for a given date.

Primary Benefits:

**1. Simplicity:** Easily extract the day component from a date.

**2. Data Analysis:** Useful in analyzing and categorizing data based on specific days of the month.

**3. Compatibility:** Works seamlessly with other date functions to break down date components.

---

**Step-by-Step Guide**

**Step 1:** Understand the Syntax
The syntax for the `DAY` function is:

| DAY(serial_number) |
| --- |

Where `serial_number` is the date from which you want to extract the day.

**Step 2:** Input the Formula

Select the cell where you want the result, and input the formula using the above syntax.

**Step 3:** Press Enter
After inputting the formula, press Enter to get the day of the month.

---

## Example

**Downloadable example:**
https://tinyurl.com/102-excel-functions

You have a list of dates representing invoice dates, and you want to extract the day of the month for each date to analyze which days are the most common for invoicing.

Data:

A1: Invoice Date     B1: Day of Month
A2: 2023-05-15
A3: 2023-05-22
A4: 2023-06-01

| | A | B |
|---|---|---|
| 1 | Invoice Date | Day of Month |
| 2 | 15/05/2023 | |
| 3 | 22/05/2023 | |
| 4 | 01/06/2023 | |

**Step 1:** Click on B2 to extract the day of the month for the first invoice date.

**Step 2:** Enter the following formula:

=DAY(A2)

| | A | B |
|---|---|---|
| 1 | Invoice Date | Day of Month |
| 2 | 15/05/2023 | =DAY(A2) |
| 3 | 22/05/2023 | |
| 4 | 01/06/2023 | |

**Step 3:** Drag the formula down from B2 to B4 to extract the day for the other invoice dates.

Results:

A1: Invoice Date     B1: Day of Month
A2: 2023-05-15     B2: 15
A3: 2023-05-22     B3: 22
A4: 2023-06-01     B4: 1

| | A | B |
|---|---|---|
| 1 | Invoice Date | Day of Month |
| 2 | 15/05/2023 | 15 |
| 3 | 22/05/2023 | 22 |
| 4 | 01/06/2023 | 1 |

**Advanced Tips:**

**1. Using with Other Functions:** Combine `DAY` with other date functions like `MONTH` or `YEAR` to extract different components of a date.

**2. Conditional Formatting:** Use the `DAY` function with conditional formatting to highlight specific days in a range of dates.

**3. Error Handling:** Ensure that the cells you're applying the `DAY` function to contain valid dates to avoid errors.

# Function #99 - VLOOKUP

The `VLOOKUP` function, which stands for "Vertical Lookup," is one of Excel's most popular functions. It's used to search for a value in the first column of a table range and return a value in the same row from a specified column.

Primary Benefits:

**1. Data Retrieval:** Easily pull related data from a table based on a given value.
**2. Saves Time:** Automates the process of manually searching for and matching data.
**3. Versatility:** Can be combined with other functions for more complex lookups.

---

## Step-by-Step Guide

**Step 1:** Understand the Syntax
The syntax for the `VLOOKUP` function is:

> **VLOOKUP(lookup_value, table_array,
> col_index_num, [range_lookup])**

- `lookup_value`: The value to search for in the first column of the table.
- `table_array`: The table range in which to find the data.
- `col_index_num`: The column index number from which to retrieve the value.
- `[range_lookup]`: Optional. If TRUE (or omitted), an approximate match is returned. If FALSE, an exact match is required.

> ➢ **Depending on your country, the ' , ' must be replaced by ' ; '**

**Step 2:** Input the Formula
Select the cell where you want the result, and input the formula using the above syntax.

**Step 3:** Press Enter
After inputting the formula, press Enter to get the corresponding value.

---

**Example**

**Downloadable example:**
https://tinyurl.com/102-excel-functions

You have a product list with prices, and you want to find the price of a specific product using its name.

Data:

A1: Product Name     B1: Price
A2: Apple            B2: $1.00
A3: Banana           B3: $0.50
A4: Cherry           B4: $2.00

Objective: Find the price of "Banana."

| | A | B |
|---|---|---|
| 1 | Product Name | Price |
| 2 | Apple | 1 |
| 3 | Banana | 0,5 |
| 4 | Cherry | 2 |

**Step 1:** In an empty cell (let's say D2), type "Banana" as the product you want to look up.

**Step 2:** In another cell (E2), enter the following formula:

=VLOOKUP(D2, A2:B4, 2, FALSE)

| | A | B | C | D | E | F | G |
|---|---|---|---|---|---|---|---|
| 1 | Product Name | Price | | | | | |
| 2 | Apple | 1 | | Banana | =VLOOKUP(D2;A2:B4; 2; FALSE) | | |
| 3 | Banana | 0,5 | | | | | |
| 4 | Cherry | 2 | | | | | |

**Step 3:** Press Enter.

Results:

D2: Banana          E2: $0.50

| | A | B | C | D | E | F |
|---|---|---|---|---|---|---|
| 1 | Product Name | Price | | | | |
| 2 | Apple | 1 | | Banana | 0,5 | |
| 3 | Banana | 0,5 | | | | |
| 4 | Cherry | 2 | | | | |
| 5 | | | | | | |

---

**Advanced Tips:**

**1. Error Handling:** If `VLOOKUP` doesn't find the lookup value, it will return an #N/A error. You can handle this using the `IFERROR` function.

**2. Approximate Match:** If you use TRUE or omit the `[range_lookup]` argument, ensure your table array's first column is sorted in ascending order.

**3. Limitations:** `VLOOKUP` only looks from left to right. If your lookup value isn't in the first column, consider using the `INDEX` and `MATCH` functions together.

---

# Function #100 - LARGE

The `LARGE` function is a tool that allows users to find the nth largest value in a dataset. Whether you're trying to identify the top three sales figures or the second highest score in a test, `LARGE` can help you achieve this with ease.

Primary Benefits:

**1. Ranking Data:** Easily identify top-performing values without sorting the entire dataset.
**2. Dynamic Analysis:** Quickly change the "n" value to analyze different positions.
**3. Versatility:** Can be combined with other functions for more advanced data analysis.

---

### Step-by-Step Guide

**Step 1:** Understand the Syntax
The syntax for the `LARGE` function is:

| **LARGE(array, k)** |
|---|

- `array`: The set of data from which you want to retrieve the nth largest value.

- `k`: The position from the largest value you wish to find (e.g., 1 for the largest, 2 for the second largest, and so on).

> ➢ **Depending on your country, the ' , ' must be replaced by ' ; '**

**Step 2:** Input the Formula
Select the cell where you want the result, and input the formula using the above syntax.

**Step 3:** Press Enter
After inputting the formula, press Enter to display the nth largest value.

---

## Example

**Downloadable example:**
https://tinyurl.com/102-excel-functions

You have a list of sales figures for the month, and you want to identify the top three sales.

Data:

A1: Sales
A2: $500
A3: $750

A4: $300

A5: $650

A6: $800

| | A | B |
|---|---|---|
| 1 | Sales | |
| 2 | 500 | |
| 3 | 750 | |
| 4 | 300 | |
| 5 | 650 | |
| 6 | 800 | |

Objective: Find the top three sales figures.

**Step 1**: In cell B2, type "1st Highest Sale".

**Step 2**: In cell C2, enter the following formula:

=LARGE(A2:A6, 1)

| | A | B | C |
|---|---|---|---|
| 1 | Sales | | |
| 2 | 500 | | =LARGE(A2:A6; 1) |
| 3 | 750 | | |
| 4 | 300 | | |
| 5 | 650 | | |
| 6 | 800 | | |

**Step 3**: Press Enter. The result in C2 should be $800.

| ◢ | A | B | C |
|---|-------|---|-----|
| 1 | Sales | | |
| 2 | 500 | | 800 |
| 3 | 750 | | |
| 4 | 300 | | |
| 5 | 650 | | |
| 6 | 800 | | |

**Step 4:** Repeat the process for the 2nd and 3rd highest sales in cells B3 and B4 respectively, adjusting the `k` value in the formula.

Results:
B2: 1st Highest Sale    C2: $800
B3: 2nd Highest Sale    C3: $750
B4: 3rd Highest Sale    C4: $650

---

**Advanced Tips:**

**1. Error Handling:** If the `k` value is greater than the number of data points in the array, `LARGE` will return a #NUM! error.

**2. Combining with Other Functions:** `LARGE` can be combined with functions like `INDEX` and `MATCH` for more advanced data retrieval tasks.

**3. Finding Smallest Values:** If you're interested in the smallest values, consider using the `SMALL` function.

---

# Function #101 - NUMBERVALUE

The `NUMBERVALUE` function is a specialized tool in Excel designed to convert text representations of numbers in a specific locale into actual numeric values. This is particularly useful when dealing with international data where decimal and group separators might differ from your local settings.

Primary Benefits:

**1. Localization:** Easily convert numbers from different locales to a standard format.
**2. Data Cleaning:** Convert text numbers to actual numeric values for calculations.
**3. Versatility:** Specify custom decimal and group separators for conversion.

---

## Step-by-Step Guide

Step 1: Understand the Syntax
The syntax for the `NUMBERVALUE` function is:

NUMBERVALUE(text, [decimal_separator], [group_separator])

- `text`: The text representation of the number you want to convert.
- `decimal_separator` (optional): The character used as a decimal separator in the text number.
- `group_separator` (optional): The character used as a group separator in the text number.

> ➤ **Depending on your country, the ' , ' must be replaced by ' ; '**

**Step 2:** Input the Formula
Select the cell where you want the result, and input the formula using the above syntax.

**Step 3:** Press Enter
After inputting the formula, press Enter to display the converted number.

---

## Example

You have received sales data from a European colleague. The numbers are formatted with a comma as the decimal separator and a period as the group separator, like "1.234,56" which represents 1,234.56 in standard U.S. format.

Data:

A1: Sales (EUR)
A2: 1.234,56
A3: 7.890,12


Objective: Convert the European formatted numbers to standard numeric values.

**Step 1:** In cell B2, type "Converted Sales".

**Step 2:** In cell C2, enter the following formula:

=NUMBERVALUE(A2, ",", ".")

**Step 3:** Press Enter. The result in C2 should be 1234.56.

**Step 4:** Drag the formula down to convert other numbers in the list.

Results:

B2: Converted Sales    C2: 1234.56
B3:                 C3: 7890.12

**Advanced Tips:**

**1. Error Handling:** If the text cannot be converted into a number, `NUMBERVALUE` will return a #VALUE! error.

**2. Locale Awareness:** Always be aware of the locale of your data source to ensure you're using the correct separators.

**3. Alternative Functions:** For simpler conversions without locale considerations, consider using the `VALUE` function.

# Function #102 - SWITCH

The `SWITCH` function is a logical function introduced in Excel 2016. It evaluates an expression against a list of values and returns the result corresponding to the first matching value. If there's no match, it can return an optional default value.

Primary Benefits:

**1. Simplicity:** Reduces the need for nested `IF` statements, making formulas easier to read and write.

**2. Efficiency:** Streamlines the process of evaluating multiple conditions.

**3. Flexibility:** Can handle numerous conditions without becoming overly complex.

---

## Step-by-Step Guide

**Step 1:** Understand the Syntax
The syntax for the `SWITCH` function is:

---

**SWITCH(expression, value1, result1, [value2, result2], ..., [default])**

---

- `expression`: The value or expression to be evaluated.

- `value1, value2, ...`: The values to compare against the expression.
- `result1, result2, ...`: The results to return if the expression matches the corresponding value.
- `default` (optional): The value to return if no matches are found.

> ➢ **Depending on your country, the ' , ' must be replaced by ' ; '**

**Step 2:** Input the Formula
Select the cell where you want the result, and input the formula using the above syntax.

**Step 3:** Press Enter
After inputting the formula, press Enter to display the result.

---

**Example**

**Downloadable example:**
https://tinyurl.com/102-excel-functions

You're a teacher grading exams. You want to assign a letter grade based on the score a student received.

Data:

A1: Score
A2: 85

Objective: Convert the numeric score to a letter grade.

**Step 1:** In cell B1, type "Grade".

**Step 2:** In cell B2, enter the following formula:

=SWITCH(
  A2,
  90, "A",
  80, "B",
  70, "C",
  60, "D",
  "F"
)

| | A | B | C | D | E |
|---|---|---|---|---|---|
| 1 | Score | | | | |
| 2 | 85 | =SWITCH(A2;90; "A"; 80; "B"; 70;"C"; 60; "D"; "F") | | | |

**Step 3:** Press Enter. Given the score of 85 in A2, the result in B2 should be "B".

**Step 4:** Drag the formula down to convert other scores in the list.

Results:

B1: Grade    B2: B

---

**Advanced Tips:**

**1. Error Handling:** If no matches are found and no default value is provided, `SWITCH` will return a #N/A error.

**2. Comparison:** Unlike `VLOOKUP` or `HLOOKUP`, `SWITCH` directly compares values, making it more straightforward for certain scenarios.

**3. Nested Usage:** While `SWITCH` reduces the need for nested `IF` statements, it can still be combined with other functions for more complex logic.

---

## Stay Ahead with Our Exclusive Excel Newsletter

The learning doesn't end with this guide! Join our FREE daily newsletter - Excel Best Tips and Tricks – ( https://www.linkedin.com/newsletters/excel-best-tips-and-tricks-7094586668371861504/ )which boasts over 100,000 avid followers. Dive into a reservoir of insights, tips, and advanced techniques, delivered straight to your inbox. It's not just a newsletter; it's a community of Excel enthusiasts, professionals, and experts, all united by a passion for mastering the world's most powerful spreadsheet software. Stay updated, stay ahead, and let's excel together!

Printed in Great Britain
by Amazon

33866408R00238